Religion Without God

'An excellent writer . . . Billington's book will be read with pleasure by scholars and intelligent laypeople alike. The educated twenty-first-century mind says no to God, yet we seem predisposed to religiosity by virtue of our DNA.'

Brooke N. Moore, *California State University, Chico*

'Well thought out and interesting.'

Keith Ward, *Oxford University*

'In many ways this is the best book I have come across on this topic. The author has a very wide knowledge of various religions, and writes with remarkable clarity. He faces squarely the question of how to describe and evaluate religion in non-sectarian terms, and his answers are extremely persuasive. Both committed believers and non-believers will find his work enlightening.'

John Wilson, *Senior Research Associate,*
Department of Educational Studies, Oxford University

It is often assumed, particularly in the West, that religion and atheism don't mix. In this challenging and thought-provoking book, Ray Billington repudiates that notion and demonstrates the viability and vitality of a religion without God.

The author draws on a lifetime's study of Asian religious traditions, including Zen and Taoism, and explores the religious dimensions of the encounter with nature, the arts and other people. He develops an understanding of religion which identifies the transcendental in our daily experience.

Religion Without God offers a refreshing new understanding of religion, one that recognises modern concerns about belief in God, while providing a positive agenda for the role of faith and religion in people's lives today.

Ray Billington is External Examiner in Philosophy for the European baccalaureate and an experienced and respected commentator on Eastern religion and philosophy. His books include *Understanding Eastern Philosophy*, *Living Philosophy* and *East of Existentialism*, all published by Routledge.

Religion Without God

Ray Billington

London and New York

First published 2002
by Routledge
11 New Fetter Lane, London EC4P 4EE

Simultaneously published in the USA and Canada
by Routledge
29 West 35th Street, New York, NY 10001

Routledge is an imprint of the Taylor & Francis Group

© 2002 Ray Billington

Typeset in Sabon by
M Rules
Printed and bound in Malta by
Gutenberg Press

British Library Cataloguing in Publication Data
A catalogue record for this book is available from the British
Library

Library of Congress Cataloging in Publication Data
Billington, Ray.
  Religion without God / Ray Billington.
    p. cm.
  Includes bibliographical references.
  1. Atheism. 2. Religion. I. Title.

BL2747.3 .B55 2001
200–dc21   2001049108

ISBN 0 415 21785 7 (hbk)
ISBN 0 415 21786 5 (pbk)

In Memoriam
Ninian Smart
Mentor and Maestro

We do not need to prove religion to men but to prove to them that they are religious.

George Tyrrell

Contents

Foreword   ix

1 Clearing the decks   1

2 Religion   9

3 Images of God   18

4 Why God?   31

5 Mysticism   47

6 Non-dualism in Hinduism   59

7 Buddhism   67

8 Taoism   79

9 Profane religion   91

10 Beyond good and evil   109

11 Substance without form   124

Select bibliography   140
Index   144

Foreword

In his introduction to the Salvation Army hymnbook, in which many hymns were set to the music of popular songs, William Booth asked rhetorically, 'Why should the devil have all the good tunes?' I wish in what follows to approach the situation in reverse: why should Christianity, Judaism or Islam lay sole claim to the transcendental? By what right are representatives of these three expressions of theism allowed to hold the stage whenever the need is felt to refer to what John Hick describes as 'the fifth dimension'?

And hold the stage they do, both in situations with which few are involved and those which, potentially, draw everybody in. The House of Commons begins each day with prayers conducted by a Church of England chaplain from across the road in Westminster Abbey. 'Thought for the Day' on BBC Radio 4's *Today* programme is almost invariably given by a spokesperson for the theistic view of life. Bishops play a leading part in determining the law of the land through their seats in the British Upper House. Religious education is still a compulsory subject in state schools, and as I write the government has announced increased aid (paid for by everybody's taxes) to church schools, where theistic beliefs can be freely broadcast without fear of contradiction.

The assumption behind all these practices is that when it comes to religion one must turn for guidance to those who proclaim the fact of God and are experts in interpreting his will. The more frequently people are reminded of him, it is assumed, the more willingly they are likely to accept whatever frustrations life brings them and live as his obedient servants; and the sooner this message is instilled in children, the better for all.

What has to be challenged is the assumption that only theists have anything authoritative to say on the fundamental nature of being, the purposiveness or otherwise of life, human nature and human destiny. Others to whom I refer from time to time are, happily, in the process of making this challenge publicly, and I simply offer my voice in support, without further pursuing that particular aspect of the situation. Those *in situ* must continue the fight, for example to have religious instruction removed from its status as a discrete subject in school curricula and its contents taught under the umbrella of cultural studies. (My own view is that children would be far better served by being introduced to yogic meditation on a regular basis than spending time pursuing St Paul around the Mediterranean or studying the smitings and slayings of early Israel).

It is however about the nature of religious experience that I most take issue with theists. The fact is that religion is universal and natural to *Homo sapiens*, whether it be referred to as experiencing the transcendental, the numinous, the spiritual, the mystical, or the ground of being. It has the power to lift people of all types and dimensions beyond the normal state of awareness into one which may be termed *wakened sleep*. It is the state of non-dualism which we experience when in dreamless sleep, with the extra factor that we remain awake. And I am suggesting that this heightened state can be entered into in a variety of contexts and through a range of activities. Some of the contexts are in fact world religions which encourage people to enter this experience primarily through meditation. They are discussed in Chapters 6, 7 and 8. Beyond the confines of these schools are areas, described in Chapter 9, which are not normally viewed as religious, yet produce experiences of religion which are, I suggest, just as real as those described by the mystics of the theistic churches.

This is bad news for anyone who believes in God as the sole source of religion, unless, like the mystics discussed in Chapter 5, it is in the unknown, unknowable and, above all, undiscussable God*head* that belief is expressed. But most theists are not mystics and their God is their own construct. This issue is discussed in Chapters 3 and 4, and the conclusion reached is that this construct has long since outlived its usefulness and should be abandoned as detrimental to genuine religious experience. This will take time, but if religion is to be rescued from God we must begin to change thought-patterns in which it too felicitously occurs. In particular, we must stop introducing it to children, whether as a warning against error or as an incentive to higher achieving. We need, quite simply, to grow up; that way, we shall be more capable of being in tune with the infinite which has no form but is a state which, entered into on an occasional basis, gives meaning to the rest of what life involves.

I hope, therefore, that the argument presented in these chapters will provide ammunition to those who wish to have all reference to God removed from public life, so that, among other benefits, people may call themselves religious without feeling that they are thereby inviting others to imprison them mentally in some kind of holy straitjacket.

My indebtedness to a host of thinkers will be obvious to any reader, but I must express special thanks to my partner Hatti Pegram for her contribution to the book: not for the ideas alone (though she will recognise some of her thoughts in what follows) but for her drive. Without it, I should still be contemplating and revising the book in my mind, worried that it would never attain the Platonic ideal. Add to that her uncomplaining acceptance of all the daily chores during the writing, and we have in her a perfect balance of the yang and the yin: a balance also shown by Mufti the cat, with her unique way of reminding me of the time to work and the time to stop. More will be heard of her elsewhere.

Note: The events of 11 September 2001 occurred as the book was going to press, and one can only guess at the further horrors which may have taken place by the time it appears in public. Suffice it to say that if, as at this point seems likely, the culprits are found to have been people whose deep sense of injustice and hatred of the USA has been fanned by religious fanaticism, then nothing that follows is affected. Genuine religion – the experience of the numinous – opens to people a spiritual dimension which both enlightens and purifies. Man-made religion creates a God with all the human strengths and weaknesses – the prejudices as well as the insights. It sees these prejudices confirmed in various man-made writings which are lifted above criticism of any kind by accepting that they are of divine origin. There is then created an indifference to the expenditure of life in this world – whether one's own or other people's – with the promise of a life in heaven which is both richer and infinitely more pleasurable than anything which this world can afford. Fundamentalism, in whichever Faith it occurs, is not religion but bigotry based on superstition. It is a disease which kills.

Chapter I

Clearing the decks

Oh what tangled webs we weave when first we practise to believe.
(Walter Scott, adaptation by Laurence Peter)

'God' is the most abused and overused word in the English language. Other words may emerge from time to time to rival it for a while, but their popularity is ephemeral in comparison. 'God save the Queen', the British sing on formal occasions; 'in God we trust' proclaims the American dollar; 'God bless us, everyone', we echo Tiny Tim and, less innocently, 'I'll have his blood, God help me'. Natural catastrophes are termed in legal documents as 'acts of God'; when asked a conjectural question the most convinced materialist may well reply, 'God knows'; 'Oh my God', people (usually non-believers) say at crucial moments; and the film director Buñuel crowned it all by declaring, tongue-in-cheek, 'I'm an atheist, thank God'. 'God' seems to be as essential to the language as salt to the sea or oxygen to the air.

Of course, this is not to say that the idea of God has been universally accepted. Although the majority of the populace may well have given their support, tacit or otherwise, to a belief in his existence (as they still do, according to all contemporary surveys), voices have been raised expressing considerable, and in some cases total, scepticism on the matter. In the field of philosophy, for instance, while some, such as Aquinas, Scotus, Ockham, Spinoza, Berkeley and Kant, expressed confidence in his existence (even if the God they envisaged was not that of the theistic creeds), others, particularly over the past three or four centuries, have openly expressed doubts on the matter or have rejected the whole concept as irrational and unworthy of consideration. Among this group are Hobbes, Hume, Mill and Russell (to name a British philosopher from each of the last four centuries).

The most belligerent of God's opponents among the philosophers was Nietzsche, with his proclamation of the death of God:

> Where is God gone? I mean to tell you! We have killed Him – you and
> I! . . . God is dead! God remains dead! And we have killed Him!
> (*The Gay Science*)

Whether Nietzsche coined that vivid phrase autonomously or had come
across it elsewhere is uncertain. It was used in 1854 by Gérard de Nerval in
his *Les Chimères* (Chimeras, or Myths):

> Dieu est mort! le ciel est vide – Pleurez! enfants, vous n'avez plus de père.
> [God is dead! Heaven is empty – Weep! children, you no longer have a
> father.]

It was Nietzsche's use of the idea which had the lasting impact, however, even
if it took nearly a century to become an in-house phrase. This happened with
the Death of God controversy in the early 1960s, inspired by the impact of
existentialist thought (chiefly Kierkegaard, Nietzsche, Heidegger and Sartre)
on the English-speaking world. In that decade, writers whose background lay
primarily in theology were challenging what seemed to many confused readers like kicking the ground from under their own feet. John Robinson,
Bishop of Woolwich, published his *Honest to God* in 1963, in which he
famously rejected the concept of a God 'out there' in favour of 'the ground
of being'. His article in the *Observer* newspaper, 'Our image of God must
go', presented the issue to an even wider audience. Other titles were even
more explicit in their rejection of the God image. Tom Altizer published his
Gospel of Christian Atheism (1966) in New York; and in 1971 Penguin
published Alistair Kee's *The Way of Transcendence*, subtitled *Christian Faith
without Belief in God*. The significant aspect of these writings is that they
were penned not by disgruntled secularists or fervent materialists, but by
people whose ambience, the context of their lives, was confessedly Christian.
In the past decade further examples have sprung from the same stable. They
include Karen Armstrong's *History of God*, published in 1993, and described
by A. N. Wilson as: 'the most fascinating and learned survey of the biggest
wild goose chase in history – the quest for God.' Wilson himself contributed
inimitably to the discussion with his *God's Funeral* (1998) – a natural sequel
to the death of God; and for a quarter of a century Don Cupitt has been
exploring the future of Christianity (in particular) with such works as *The
Sea of Faith* (1984), which led to the formation of a body of Christians under
that name, some of them exploring how far their faith could withstand the
demise of God, and *After God* (1997) which seeks, in the author's words, 'a
new theory of the twilight of the gods'.

The historical developments which cradle and inspire these enquiries can
be traced back to the Renaissance, when scholars first began to challenge
across a broad spectrum the God-centred doctrines which had been the
required focus of previous explorations. Wilson, in particular, has pinpointed

some of the most eminent thinkers over the past half-millennium who have tried to come to terms with life without God.

The supreme catalyst in this field has been the advance of science which, despite the affirmation by many of its pioneers that they remained believers, has effectively appeared to make God redundant by offering a naturalistic account of what had previously been held to be miraculous. We can identify three major steps in this process. The first, after the invention of the telescope, followed the astronomical discoveries of Copernicus and Galileo. The cosy picture of the earth as the centre of the universe, with *Homo sapiens* as its guardian under God, had to go: the solar system could be explained without the hand of God. The second, two centuries later, was the biological revolution culminating in Darwin's *The Origin of Species*, arguably the most important, if most unread, book ever penned. Those who, no longer able to accept the God of 'the spacious firmament on high', had turned to the one who had made 'all things bright and beautiful' and of whom they could sing 'All things praise thee, Lord most high', were now brought face to face with Tennyson's 'nature, red in tooth and claw'; with the realisation that all its manifestations were brought about by trial and error rather than purposiveness; with Tom and Jerry rather than the lion lying down with the lamb. The effect of this teaching was to make God redundant in the evolution of species. We shall study in Chapter 9 the sense of awe, mystery and mysticism which nature evokes; but it is a sense which is totally independent of – and is in some ways repugnant to – the concept that, where nature's manifestations are concerned, 'the Lord God made them all'.

Where, then, was God to be found? The later Victorians turned their attention to the inner light and identified God as the voice of their consciences. To whatever extent creation and evolution could be satisfactorily explained without recourse to a divine instigator, nothing, surely, could remove him from the inner self. Then, in the early decades of the twentieth century, arrived the psychoanalysts with, in particular, Freud's teaching about the unconscious mind, suggesting that the idea of the conscience as the still small voice of God must go, to be replaced by that of an accumulation of experiences and ideas encountered at all stages of any individual person's life, which may be forgotten but never lost.

In our own time, study of our genetic structure and, in particular, the discovery of the human genome, have thrown the question of God's place in human life into even more intense relief. If we can now choose not only what sex we wish our children to be, but also whether they should be dark or fair, tall or short, brainy or just average, healthy or taking their chances as in the past, what role is left for God?

There are two problems facing anyone who is looking for an answer to this dilemma. First, as is indicated in every opinion poll about God's possible existence, while church-going is clearly on the decline, about seventy per cent of the British population (more in the USA) express a belief in God, even if it is no more than 'a God of some sort'. As one participant in a televised teach-in on the subject stated, 'Well, there must be someone there, mustn't there, else how did it all come into being?' – unwittingly (perhaps) outlining the cosmological argument for his existence. Belief in God's existence is expressed more fervently in the United States than in other Western countries, frequently from the viewpoint of the conservative evangelicals or biblical fundamentalists. It is an astonishing fact that in 1999, a century and a quarter after the publication of *The Origin of Species*, one of the states of the USA (Kansas) banned the teaching of evolution in its schools on the grounds that it was anti-scriptural, alien to the so-called 'Word of God' (one of the most potently destructive phrases in the language, as will be illustrated later). Many other states insist that the myth of biblical creationism be taught alongside the 'theory' of evolution, but to ban it totally meant a return to the so-called 'monkey trial' in Tennessee in 1926, when a teacher was found guilty in court of propagating this scientific 'heresy'. So to suggest – as I shall do – that the time has come for *Homo sapiens* to dispense with the idea of God *in toto*, whether we're referring to the Jewish Jehovah, the Christian Father of Jesus Christ, or the Islamic Allah, is to court trouble. But courted it must be.

The second problem springs from the first. With an overwhelming majority of the human race confessedly believing in God (even though the percentage is considerably lower among those aged below thirty) we're looking at not only an enormous number but also a wide range of people: rich and poor, black and white, scholarly and illiterate, sophisticated and simple, cultured and superstitious. Inevitably, with such a range of believers, the concept which is believed in varies considerably. In fact, if it were possible to gather into one volume what people mean when they express a belief in God, the cornucopia of descriptions must challenge, if not totally defy, the kind of analysis on which we are embarking. Yet some sort of analysis is essential if the discussion is to be any more than a sequence of vague generalities.

Ironically, one of the main grounds for dispensing with the word God altogether is the very fact that it is laden with such a superabundance of meanings, many of them mutually contradictory. It is possible, for example, to hear one person say 'I don't believe in God' and another 'I believe in God' and so reach the conclusion that they are on opposite sides on the matter. On analysis, however, it could be found that the non-believer is actually denying belief in the almighty-being-in-the-sky, the heavenly father who 'holds the whole world in his hand', while the second is simply affirming a disbelief in any kind of God 'out there', but would not reject what has been termed a 'ground of being' in which his life is focused – that is, a basic motivation or drive which inspires him to get on with his daily duties: a belief with which the first speaker might well be in total agreement. In any other sphere of human thought such a state of affairs would be viewed as ludicrous, confusing, and even potentially dangerous: yet it seems to be tolerated in religion.

What is required, then, is not just a process of linguistic analysis – though that must be included – but an examination of what people have in mind when they speak about God – or god, or gods. Granted that many use it mindlessly – 'my God, it's broken' is hardly an act of prayer or a declaration of faith – there are manifestly huge numbers of people who could give some kind of explanation both of what 'God' means in general and of what he means to them in particular. Further, although no two accounts would be exactly the same, a number of ideas would surely recur (it would be remarkable, with such a subject, if this were not the case) from which could be extrapolated some core concepts, which become the central themes of a valid enquiry or analysis. It may not be possible to write QED at the end of the enquiry, but it will at least be one conducted without vagueness as to terms of reference.

To make such an assessment as comprehensive as possible, a number of perspectives will be necessary. This will of course include the scientific, but this is only the beginning of the story. Over the past century there has been increased communication with the East, and consequently a deepening of understanding of the religions which have played a dominant role in creating its varied cultural traditions: Hinduism, Buddhism and Taoism, for example. The fact that God plays no part in a large proportion of these religious beliefs is highly significant and often overlooked by the increasing numbers in the West who are turning to these religions for some kind of insights deeper than the shallow – as they view it – capitalist philosophy which pervades the air they breathe, pollutes the water they drink and poisons the life-giving earth. It is often considered that to reject God is to embrace this materialist outlook because it appears that by rejecting him the unbeliever is also rejecting spiritual values in favour of earthly treasures, dedicating his/her life to what the Hindus term *maya*, illusion. This misconception must be nipped in the bud.

In its turn this leads to a consideration of the other key word used in this book. The word 'religion', even if not as broadly as the word God, has a plethora of connotations and manifestations. Mussolini described fascism as a religion; Aneurin Bevan said the same of socialism; Keats of love. These examples water the word down to such an extent that it becomes difficult to discern anything distinctive in it. If, for example, our chief interest is our religion, then we're all religious, whether we're football enthusiasts, physical fitness fanatics, sexual athletes or crossword buffs. I shall be trying to illustrate that being religious is a condition shared by many more than those who express a belief in God; but it doesn't include everybody, despite Samuel Butler's assertion: 'To be at all is to be religious more or less'.

My primary concern lies with the essential difference between the 'more' and the 'less', and what it is that brings about the difference. Certainly, there are some human experiences with their associated activities which some people have described as religious, even though they take place in different contexts from those usually considered to be religious (such as places of worship). These spheres include, in particular, the arts and a reverence for nature. Some remarks made to Beethoven toward the end of his life illustrate how smoothly music slots into this category. His friend Karl Peters wrote to him in 1823: 'Granted that you don't believe in [immortality] you will be glorified, because your music [is] religion.' Others have expressed similar convictions about poetry, drama and imaginative literature, about painting and sculpture. For these people, to be in thrall to a work of art is, I shall suggest, a religious experience, producing a profound sense of awe. We may not be able to analyse the nature of artistic achievement (Freud described it as 'psychologically inaccessible'), but we can learn from Henry Moore when he said of his sculpting that he could 'really be in control, almost like God creating something'.

The same intensity of feeling has frequently overtaken people when communing with nature. Wordsworth's 'Lines Composed a Few Miles Above Tintern Abbey', which I shall discuss on pp. 101–2, suggests that the poet was undergoing a religious experience and that the poem is a religious poem. Those committed to the God hypothesis may well describe both these spheres as channels through which God reveals himself; but this is to add a superfluous concept, and I shall be suggesting that art and nature are real expressions of what Dietrich Bonhoeffer described as 'the beyond in the midst'. Whatever religion is, it certainly includes a sense of the reality of this experience.

But this is already jumping several guns. We need to investigate the meaning of the word religion – no straightforward task, as sociologists and psychologists, as well as theologians, know full well. But since my purpose, indicated in the title, is to retain the religious element in human experience without recourse to God, an examination of the word and its usage is essential. The position adopted in what follows may be described as somewhere between the materialistic stance (in its strictly philosophical sense that only matter is real) and the theological, in its etymological sense as writings about, or understanding of, God. There are theologians who don't believe in God, certainly not in the traditional sense of that phrase. Don Cupitt is one, and the organisation which he founded, the Sea of Faith, regularly explores this way of thinking in its journal. It is in fact now quite possible to study theology while remaining devoutly atheistic, which I don't recall of any fellow-student when I first tackled the subject. But it will make for greater clarification if the word theology is used in its original sense (its *Urbedeutung*, as the Germans would say) so that its denotation can be contrasted with that of religion without causing confusion.

With this in mind, the purpose of this book can be simply stated: it is to rid religion of theology, to rescue it from God, to declare God redundant. It requires us to look anew at our cultural and natural heritage, and to appreciate that the religious experience is one that is potentially available to everyone without their having to make obeisance in the direction of the supernatural. Religion is not a gift bestowed upon grateful receivers by an act of revelation from on high: it is a natural part of human experience which embraces many more people than actually claim to be religious. I shall in fact be suggesting that belief in the God hypothesis is not per se an expression of religion at all: for many of the alleged eighty per cent who express belief in him it is no more than a superstition which, *inter alia*, indicates a lack of willingness either to think, or accept responsibility, for themselves.

There are a number of practical implications for anyone who advocates the removal of God from our thought and speech processes, and they are discussed in the latter stages of what follows. There is, first of all, the problem of what, if anything, we are to put in his place, bearing in mind Chesterton's wry comment that if people don't believe in God, they won't believe in nothing – they'll believe in anything. With the growing popularity of New Age concepts, and the (less desirable) proliferation of cults of various kinds, this stricture cannot be ignored. Most of the cults are directed towards a charismatic person (usually male) who seems able to achieve a remarkable control of people's minds, and who exploits this power unashamedly. The result is the phenomenon of people laying aside all common sense and abandoning themselves to outbursts of unbridled emotion which, at least for one who has witnessed such displays, are offensively subhuman. Whatever may emerge as the essence of religious experience, and acknowledging that the human faculty of reason is not broad enough in its scope to contain the whole of – or even to explain – that experience, reason must not be cast aside. Religion may be super-rational: it is not irrational, as Wittgenstein affirmed when he described his mind-blowing investigations into logic as a religious activity.

A further problem is the sociological and cultural hold that God still exerts. As already stated, parliament in Britain begins daily with prayers, seeking his blessing on the day's proceedings (a triumph of optimism over experience, perhaps). God's strength is invoked at the crowning of monarchs, and his comfort at their funerals. Societies up and down the land – Friendly Societies, Masonic Lodges, self-help groups such as Alcoholics Anonymous, school assemblies – invoke his wisdom in their activities. A larger number of people than attend church services take their offspring to church for baptism and their deceased relatives for burial; church marriages remain popular even among people whose only link with the place is that it's the particular church they stay away from; and at Christmas millions of people the length and breadth of the land sing lustily:

> He came down to earth from heaven,
> Who is God and Lord of all.

No wonder Nietzsche commented:

> God is dead: but considering the state the species Man is in, there will perhaps be caves, for ages yet, in which his shadow will be shown.

The question arises: what do we tell the children? Many parents feel that religious education is valuable for their offspring, not for its theoretical content but because there seems to be no other viable context for the laying down of moral guidelines – yet the alleged link between God's will and moral behaviour has been challenged for centuries, not just by philosophers but by churchmen. A noted example is Richard Holloway, former Bishop of Edinburgh, who has embarked into this battlefield – which for some remains a minefield – with his book *Godless Morality – Keeping Religion out of Ethics* (1999). There is nothing new in this aspiration, of course: Hume was saying the same a quarter of a millennium ago; but its implications must be re-examined in the present context.

All this stripping away needs some kind of forecast of its implications for the future of God-centred religion. Difficult though it is to play the prophet in this sphere, some attempt must be made if this book is to be more than a mere expression of hope, pious or otherwise, of what might be. Daydreaming will not do in a world where we are constantly charged to 'get real'. There have been plenty of analyses of past developments and current trends where God is concerned, often expressed in words and with references which only the initiated can understand. Here, I wish to express, as simply as possible, what religion really is, and encourage many who had not thought of themselves as religious to view at least some of their experiences of life in that way. The key requirement in this process is to remove the concept of God. We need mysticism without theology.

Chapter 2

Religion

A man's religion is the chief fact with regard to him

(Carlyle)

Like all words which relate to human experiences and accomplishments – art, education, philosophy, politics are typical examples – religion does not lend itself to any kind of simplistic definition. It can, of course, mean a particular system of belief or worship, such as Judaism, Buddhism or Shintoism, but if that were the whole story it would be a relatively simple matter to attain a picture of what religion 'means': one would merely have to describe how each religion operates, describe its beliefs and practices, perhaps compare and contrast one with another, and emerge with a reasonably comprehensive delineation of religions as we observe them. But this would be too facile a process: it gives, perhaps, an account which can be readily understood, but only because the field is kept too circumscribed. It may produce a meaning of religion, but only one of the many that would emerge if the field were extended and the terms of reference broadened out. To study formal religions as they present themselves may, in fact, not even draw out the most important meaning, or meanings, of the word because religion is not just a system, but a personal experience involving some kind of commitment. As C. G. Jung wrote:

> So long as religion is only faith and outward form, and the religious function is not experienced in our own souls, nothing of any importance has happened.
>
> (*Psychology and Alchemy*, 1953)

This begs the question, which will be discussed in Chapter 11, of the meaning of the ambiguous word 'soul', but Jung provides a clear signpost for this enquiry: religion is personal; it is within us, consciously *or otherwise*.

Etymologically the word derives from the Latin *religio* (adjective *religiosus*): but with what is that word connected? The link is often made with *religare*, meaning to bind, but even that is ambiguous: bound to what, to whom? One could say that anything to which a person is *bound* will play a dominant role in his or her life. Thus the pursuit of learning could be one man's religion, and numerous scholars might well concur: but, by the same token, the cultivation of idleness could be another's. For some, it is the desire to 'pass our days in rest and quietness', as the Prayer Book puts it; others prefer the whiff of battle in their nostrils, another mountain to climb, a new cause to champion. For countless members of the human race, football is then a religion, sex is a religion, helping the poor and the distressed is a religion, war is a religion, making money is a religion: anything, in fact, which a person thinks about most in his or her spare time.

Clearly, whatever definition, or definitions, of religion we settle for, it can be taken as a factor that plays at least a compelling part in the life of anyone who pursues it, and perhaps an all-absorbing one. It would be not a little odd for anyone to say, 'Music is my religion, but I hardly ever listen to it', or 'Alcohol is my religion, but I only drink on Saturday nights'. But is it enough to content ourselves with this loose, even amorphous, definition? If all obsessions, enthusiasms, areas of deep personal commitment constitute a person's religion, why have the word at all? Would we not be wiser, if only for the sake of linguistic accuracy, to dispense with it altogether, as W. C. Smith proposed in *The Meaning and End of Religion*, written in 1964 while the 'Honest to God' controversy was raging? This might offer the relief of a reprieve, but the respite would surely be brief. The fact is that a fair percentage of the human race accept (most of them tacitly, to be sure, but that will suffice to make the point) that there is a distinction to be made between the religious experience and the experiences that accrue from the enthusiastic pursuit of pleasurable activities. Even though I shall from time to time be suggesting (especially in Chapter 9) modifications in this vox pop distinction, Smith's recommendation that 'religion' be declared redundant on the grounds that its interpretations are too numerous seems to be a case of throwing out the gold dust with the grit.

Even Smith made one exemption, *personal piety*, from the features which he wished to exclude from any association with religion. But piety will hardly do, since it simply raises further questions with regard to its nature, its manifestation and, above all, its direction. With what, to return to *religare*, is piety *bound*? It will show itself in the exercise of self-control (from the Greek *egkrateia*, meaning, literally, making oneself thin, or holding oneself in) which would appear to exclude from the arena of religion anyone who has a lust for life. This seems, at the very least, anti-evolutionary.

It may help if we return to the first definition outlined on p. 9 and explore the characteristics frequently associated with a religion. This won't tell us comprehensively what it is to be religious, but it should help to shed some light on what Ovid termed the 'rough and disorderly mass'.

As a start, I shall use a well-known list of characteristics of religion offered by W. P. Alston in his book *Philosophy of Language*. He makes nine suggestions:

1 Belief in supernatural beings (gods).
2 A distinction between sacred and profane objects.
3 Ritual acts focused around sacred objects.
4 A moral code believed to be sanctioned by the gods.
5 Characteristically religious feelings (awe, sense of mystery, sense of guilt, adoration, etc.), which tend to be aroused in the presence of sacred objects and during the practice of ritual, and which are associated with the gods.
6 Prayer and other forms of communication with gods.
7 A world view, that is, a general picture of the world as a whole and of the place of the individual in it, including a specification of its overall significance. [Alston presumably includes in this characteristic a belief in some kind of continuing existence after the end of this life, or, in Hindu terminology, cycle of experience (samsara).]
8 A more or less total organisation of one's life based on the world view.
9 A social organisation bound together by the preceding characteristics.

To these, and thinking along similar lines, I should wish to add:

10 The acceptance of certain texts as being inspired by God, so that they exemplify the distinction made in 2; may be seen as the main source of the knowledge of 4; are read publicly in the context of 3, and privately as an expression of 6.

Two points can be made immediately. First, some of the world religions either treat as unimportant or disregard entirely some of these characteristics. Only the theistic religions (Judaism, Christianity and Islam) accept that there is a connection between how I feel I ought to behave (4) and obeying the will of God. In India, Jainism and Buddhism, particularly in the Theravada expression, and in China, in Taoism and Confucianism, the idea of God is either ignored or rejected, and with it much of what is included under 5, together with 2 – the distinction between sacred and profane objects. This is a point of view shared by arguably the most religiously advanced (though that value judgment must be discussed later) system in Hinduism, Advaita Vedanta. Though teaching that the union between the self (Atman) and the ground of being (Brahman) is the moment of enlightenment, Vedanta does not view this as a supernatural experience, but rather as the end of all *human* endeavour, and therefore as a thoroughly natural, though not universally experienced (at any rate not in this life) happening. (The word supernatural is another of the vague terms which must be examined in more detail later.) Zen Buddhists and, among Christians, Quakers and Salvationists have only a modicum of ritual in their religious activities, and numerous hermits, mystics and other contemplatives over the centuries have had little to do with any social organisation, often being treated with suspicion by those who do. It seems that the manifestation of the characteristics which Alston outlines has been a pick-and-mix affair so far as the world's religions are concerned.

The second area of discussion arising from the list springs from the fact that a host of people belong to organisations which would normally be categorised under the umbrella of secular rather than religious, yet still evince many of the characteristics that Alston describes. These include bodies or clubs whose interests focus on the academic, political, social, cultural and sporting. Let's take just one example – the supporters' club of a professional football team. Fans may not believe in the God as proclaimed in local churches, but will treat the key members of their team – and with some clubs like Manchester United *all* its members – as at least demigods. Souvenir programmes, especially those gained in exotic places or on occasions of great triumphs, together with other memorabilia of the club, are treated with a reverence which would seem to reflect a sense of the sacred. Club meetings will follow a certain invariable pattern which becomes fixed and ritualistic – a ritual which is continued on the terraces as club choruses, even hymns, perhaps – are chanted by the devotees. Supporters will be expected to be suitably deferential in their attitude to club personnel and property, and – though this is often less obvious – to behave themselves on the terraces. Awe towards the club and its history, adoration of its players and manager, guilt at failing to support the team on certain occasions, reflect the 'characteristic religious feelings'. Prayer is expressed in the voluble support for the team during a game, prayers of exculpation when they lose and of thanksgiving when they win, so that a liturgist could well use their emotions as a case study. The world view is simple and basic: the team is the best in the land or – if we are to refer again to Manchester United – in the world. Genuine fans will spend virtually all their spare time either thinking or talking about the club, or attending meetings, or going to matches near and far; and will gladly sacrifice all their spare cash in the process. The club is the social organisation, and the club's magazine (fanzine), together with newspaper reports about the team's doings, provide its scriptures. Thus we find all the characteristics of a religion (some, admittedly, more obvious than others) in a football club. It seems that we must conclude either that Alston's list, especially No. 9, is too broadly based (or is frankly wrong) or that our view and definition of religion must be changed.

It should help the enquiry if, as a working hypothesis, we could achieve by a process of elimination some kind of consensus as to which of the ten features are a sine qua non of religion and which can be included on a take-it-or-leave-it basis. On this basis I think we can immediately exclude three of Alston's suggestions (Nos 2, 3 and 4), together with the one that I added. It is not essential to distinguish between sacred and profane objects; otherwise, to give one small but significant example, the Quakers, members of the Society of Friends, could not be described as religious. Their rejection of the sacraments of baptism and holy communion springs from their conviction that everything in life is sacred, and that to state otherwise is to fall into 'the scandal of the particular': the view that some things, and some people, have a special hold on sacredness which separates them from others of their kind. For that reason they have no priests, believing instead in the priesthood of all believers. If no distinction is made between the sacred and the secular, it follows that there will be no ritual focused on sacred objects. The centrality of this characteristic of religion is, in fact, more widely rejected than the first, since there are plenty of people who assert their religious convictions without engaging themselves in any kind of related communal worship. Zen Buddhism actually warns its devotees that ritual is generally harmful to real religion, since outward observances can easily be mistaken for inner meaning or reality; and Hinduism, in its triumvirate of major *obstacles* to the attaining of *moksha* (enlightenment) includes *dharma* – religious rules and observances – alongside *artha* (wealth) and *kama* (desire). It has been well said (though the pun is not so effective in Sanskrit) that many a man prays on his knees on the Sabbath and on his neighbours for the rest of the week.

With equal confidence we can sideline two related characteristics: the moral code believed to be sanctioned by the gods, and the acceptance of supernaturally inspired texts which are held to be the main source of instruction as to the code's content. There are enough thinking and concerned people in the world, and enough non-religious societies – humanist, secular – among whom moral and social values are subjects of deep reflection and even anguish to make these the most easily dispensable of all allegedly religious characteristics. Many committed members of the theistic religions, in fact, find no problem with this dispensation, as is illustrated in Bishop Holloway's stance, already mentioned. Eastern religions are quite indifferent to what has been termed in the West 'the morality of divine commands'. For example, at the heart of the moral teaching of the Chinese philosophy of Taoism is the admonition not to obey the will of God (or of the Tao) but to be natural. Confucius, while often referring to 'the way of heaven', uses the phrase as a synonym for the best as we understand it; and Hinduism and Buddhism both offer their moral injunctions as guidelines rather than a formal code, a piece of advice from those who are aware of the moral pitfalls ahead rather than a take-them-or-suffer-the-consequences set of injunctions from a God who, having made the rules up, has the absolute authority to lay the law down.

The rejection of divinely inspired texts is a corollary of the view that 'I ought' means 'God wills', and it is the theistic religions which face the tallest hurdle here. The treatment of their scriptures as the word of God has been their rock in more senses than one: a rock can both give a firm foundation and destroy whatever and whoever founders on it. True, the Hindus have their Vedas, Buddhists their Dharmapada, Taoists their *Tao Te Ching* and Confucians the Analects. However, the authority of these classics lies not in their origin but in the length of time (up to four millennia for the Vedas) that they have proved inspirational to their readers. But to be inspirational is different from being supernaturally inspired, otherwise the cricketers' *Wisden* or the 'big book' of Alcoholics Anonymous must be given equal status. Both these issues – the link between morals and religion and the importance of sacred texts – are important for our enquiry and will be considered at greater length in Chapter 10; for the present it is enough to deny that they are essential to a religion, in the sense that without them it would lose its *raison d'être*.

The characteristics outlined in the middle block of Alston's list cannot be assessed so straightforwardly. Clearly, his description of religious feelings (5) could be dispensed with if he had implied that they tend to be aroused *only* in the presence of sacred objects or during ritual since, as we have seen, these factors are not viewed as essential to a religion. Nor should it be retained if the examples of the relevant feelings imply obeisance and humility before a God such as the theistic religions proclaim (the sense of guilt and adoration are the examples Alston uses). However, whatever the ultimate definition of religion may be, it is unlikely to exclude the subject's feelings. It would be difficult to take seriously any person who confessed himself to be religious, but felt nothing in particular about it (along the lines described by a student of mine who began an essay on yoga with the words, 'My aunt has no problem with her yoga: she fits it in between her sauna and her bridge'). No doubt there are adherents of all the world's religions who are dispassionate to the point of being soulless (if that word doesn't beg too many questions at this stage) about their religion, but they are seldom likely to be more than also-rans in the religious stakes. A sense of awe and, especially, mystery seem natural concommitants in this field: it is, after all, an indication of the mysterious nature of the subject that makes any exploration into its meaning, such as this present exercise, both tortuous and hazardous. It seems reasonable, therefore, to retain some of Alston's 'characteristic feelings' (the sense of awe and mystery) as essential to religion, together with cognate feelings such as wonder, fascination and, perhaps, ecstasy. But these should be accepted without reference to specific places, objects or events designated as sacred as opposed to profane, which are suggested in the other half of Alston's categorisation.

The next characteristic presupposes a belief in 'the gods', or, presumably, God. As it stands, it must therefore be excluded from the list of essential features, since neither Taoism, Jainism, nor several schools of Buddhism generally refer to either God or gods or, if they do, pay little or no regard to him/her/them. This feature could be less contentiously incorporated if we broadened the word prayer to include meditation and contemplation. Prayer always implies an approach to someone else, whether this be God, another human being, or a court of justice. Prayers can be answered, ignored, or turned down. The process is two-way. Meditation, on the other hand, requires no second party. It is a deliberate turning away, physically and mentally, from the daily round of duties and engaging in the process of reflection. Unlike prayer, which can be a public, communal activity, meditation takes place in seclusion. 'Nowhere,' wrote Marcus Aurelius, 'can man find a quieter or more untroubled retreat than in his own soul.' Whether meditation should be viewed as simply an exploration of oneself, as Descartes affirmed in his *First Meditation* by describing it as 'holding converse only with myself', or whether it means seeking a state of absorption in something beyond oneself – the void, the ground of being, the Tao – will be discussed later: for the present it seems sufficient to say that a person's religion, even where this is expressed primarily through social or political involvement, will probably include times of meditation or reflection if only to avoid being burned out. That, at any rate, is the counsel offered by the yin–yang philosophy which we shall explore in Chapter 7. So, with another (major) modification to Alston's description, we retain his characteristic 6.

Alston's next two suggestions – the holding of a world view and the commitment of one's life to it – seem axiomatic in this context. To declare oneself to be religious is to make a metaphysical statement, which is to hold a world view (for a start, that there is such an entity as metaphysics). But there is nothing specifically religious in holding a world view, or a philosophy of life; the majority of the world's citizens have probably pondered on 'the meaning of life', even if they have concluded that it has no meaning in the sense which that phrase implies.

How deeply a religious person's life should be committed to his or her religion is a moot point: Alston uses the ambiguous phrase 'more or less' and we may accept that vague expression. It seems reasonable to expect a religious person (and what that means has yet to be determined, of course) to spend a fair amount of his or her time, energies and possessions in religious activity, but it seems unnecessary to require more. This characteristic adds little to the overall picture.

So far, then, I have suggested the following as essential to religion: the expression of certain feelings, some form of meditation or contemplation, together with what may be termed a philosophical approach to the world and the understanding of one's place in it; and the hint that these are likely to play more than a minor role in a religious person's existence. What must be obvious is that the basic issue has not been mentioned. It is Alston's first, and is pivotal to our theme.

If we are to take Alston's words at their face value, we could relegate this first-mentioned characteristic from the level of a requirement to that of an optional extra. Belief in supernatural beings, or gods, (to which the singular 'God' must clearly be added) certainly plays a major role in many religions; but by no means all, and not in the thinking of some affiliates of those where it does. Taoism speaks of 'immortals', but these are mythical figures whose longevity reflects their faithfulness to the Tao, the way; Confucius refused to speculate on such matters, arguing that people have enough trouble coping with the problems of the here and now, without speculating about anything beyond this dimension. Buddha was agnostic about the gods, suggesting that if they did exist, their condition was lower than that of those who had achieved Nirvana. Jainism rejects the concept of gods altogether, replacing belief in them with the assertion that any human being who reaches the highest level of spiritual achievement, which is the realisation of him/herself as pure knowledge (*jiva*), experiences all that could possibly be ascribed to a deity: perfect wisdom, perfect serenity. It is never possible to generalise about Hinduism, of course, since it embraces numerous systems and writings over at least two millennia, but in the teaching of Advaita Vedanta the view is expressed that the Atman (the self) and Brahman (the ground of being, or sustaining force of the universe) are essentially one and the same, and that the moment of moksha (enlightenment) is when this truth is understood. Thus the great non-dualistic affirmation *tat tvam asi* ('thou art that', where 'that' is the universal and eternal spirit) can also be translated 'I am that', or 'all this is that', or 'there is nothing but that'. It would be far too simplistic, and alien to Hindu thought processes, to translate this statement as 'I am God'; but it is not so outrageous a claim in the Hindu context as it would seem in that of Western theism, where it would be considered megalomanic if not psychotic, its perpetrator a candidate for the asylum.

I have already quoted books by Christian authors who maintain religious beliefs, but reject the idea of and necessity for God as a feature of their religion. This rejection together with other religions' agnosticism on the matter, suggests that what Alston terms supernatural may not have to depend on the concept of a God or gods to justify its reality. And once this possibility has been accepted, we are engaging ourselves in a totally different form of thought from that which evolves from the God concept. We are, in fact, releasing ourselves from the theological perspective – one which begins with the idea of a supreme being or beings, capable of being analysed, if not anatomised in the process of specialised discourse – and are entering into a universe of spiritual experience which is made real to us not by academic debate or idealised images reflecting the perfect being or beings of our aspirations, but simply through the experiences we undergo. I am suggesting that the first characteristic offered by Alston is essential to religion, but only if we exclude any reference to God(s). The leitmotiv of this book is that he, she, it, or they belong on the discretionary list; but that does not mean that the

spiritual dimension suggested by Alston's first characteristic is similarly rel-
egated: quite the contrary, in fact. It is difficult to conceive of a religion, or
of a person who describes herself as religious, in which, or for whom, there
is no *spiritual* dimension. I shall discuss later (Chapter 9) whether this is the
correct word to use, since I shall be introducing it into areas beyond those
normally associated with religion, but it may suffice for the moment. At this
stage, it is enough to make two affirmations. First, that human experience
over the millennia suggests – some might say indicates – that the world of
metaphysics is a reality, not a fantasy, much less an aberration; and, second,
that metaphysics does not require theology – literally, knowledge of God – in
order to find a rationale.

I know that many people who still refer, or defer, to God in the religious
dimension of their lives do so without the personalised images associated
with its more primitive or fundamentalist manifestations, and are therefore
likely to describe the above not as a new perspective, but as one with which
they have lived and to which they have adapted for decades or more (with
the implication that no more needs to be added on the matter). To anyone
who thinks along such lines I would simply put the question: if it is the case
that whatever they deem to be the value of religion is capable of being
expressed without reference to God, are we not more likely to achieve a
modicum of enlightenment in the situation if we dispense with the word altogether and speak instead of what we know to be real? Martin Buber, in his
book *I and Thou* boldly stated, 'When you get to the Thou, God is no
more', a perspective which will be directly explored in Chapter 9. Buber was
perhaps unwittingly building on the *Tao Te Ching*, written some two and a
half millennia earlier, which begins with the immortal line:

The Tao that can be named is not the eternal Tao.

What that means must be explored later. Our task now is to turn to the concept of God or gods in order to be clearer about what exactly people who
have expressed a belief in him (them) have had in mind, and why the idea of
his, her, or their existence has been so important to them.

Chapter 3

Images of God

> If God made us in his own image, we have certainly returned the compliment.
>
> (Voltaire)

The aim of this book is to show that, while religion is fundamental to the human condition, God is not. Religion is natural, God is artificial; religion is unavoidable, God is redundant. Why it remains the case that people still turn to God in their millions will be the subject of the next chapter. At this stage I wish to examine what it is that people have in mind when they reflect on the idea of God, or gods. It would clearly be impossible to describe every nuance of belief without making a whole book of a single chapter, but I shall attempt to outline those concepts which are most broadly expressed. In a situation where people can speak freely of 'God as we understand him' – to quote a fixed phrase of one self-help organisation – it should not surprise anyone that even a broad canvas yields a plethora of images to compare and contrast.

Deism

While there are several forms of deism, its general use stems from the seventeenth century, the Age of Enlightenment, when science had begun to provide the authority for people to cope with the complexities of the universe without falling back on the concept of God. God was viewed by deists as one who, having created the universe (in whatever time it took: the debate on that issue was just beginning to warm up) then retired for a well-earned rest, lasting for the remainder of eternity.

There is, in fact, a certain logic in this belief. Granted that since he was perfect, he could hardly create something imperfect (unless he was being deliberately devious, like the manufacturers of obsolescent light-bulbs); it follows that the world, being a perfect product of a perfect being (how else do we know of his perfection except through the evidence of his works?), no longer requires his assistance. Deism is the product of a broad human need, which we shall examine in the next chapter, to see a purpose in and a cause of everything. With time being viewed as lineal, God is used as a shorthand term to explain what otherwise seems inexplicable. Apart from its use of God as a *deus ex machina*, deism generally avoids the concept that there is any form of direct communication between God and his creatures. He has left them to work out their own salvation, with the result that, so far as they are concerned, their experience of him is not dissimilar to that of agnostics if not atheists.

Pantheism

The etymology of this word (as with most of the others to be examined) lies in the Greek language. 'Pan' means 'all' and 'theos' means 'God'. So the core of this theory is that God is all and all is God; in fact, it would not be inapposite to transliterate pantheism as 'all-God-ism'. Many pantheists define 'all' in terms of 'all that lives' – from *Homo sapiens* to the amoeba, from the mustard seed to the oak tree. But since nothing that has being in this world can exist independently of the surroundings in which the process of being is set, some 'hard' pantheists include inanimate objects along with sentient beings, stones, rivers and mountains alongside grass, insects, birds, fish and mammals, as manifestations of God.

Among modern philosophers, nobody expressed pantheism more directly than Spinoza. In his *Ethics* (1: 18) he wrote:

> All things that are, are in God, and must be conceived through God, and therefore God is the cause of things which are in Himself. This is the first point. Further, no substance can be granted outside God, that is, nothing which is outside God exists in itself; which was the second point. Therefore God is the immanent, but not transcendent, cause of all things.

The words 'immanent' and 'transcendent' are descriptive of, on the one hand, the divine presence within us (and, for pantheists, within all other beings) and, on the other, the divine manifested through the universe 'out there'. As we saw, deists refer (and occasionally defer) to this distant God: pantheists, on the contrary, rejoice in one who is manifested in our midst, within human beings and all other creatures. Even this statement is not entirely accurate, however, since it still retains a dualistic notion (*God in me, I in God*) which is alien to the deepest pantheistic ideas. God *is* me, and I *am* God would be a more accurate statement, though, as we shall see, statements of that kind should be used with the utmost caution if their meaning is not to be distorted.

What worries many about pantheism is its lack of belief in a God with moral qualities. Its viewpoint is, in fact, a logical inference from its basic image of God. If it is the case that the divine is expressed in every living being, then, at least so far as the human examples are concerned, no moral judgment can be made on behaviour, whether it be the kind of which we usually express approval, such as goodwill, tolerance, fair play and so on, or that which usually receives condemnation such as malice, greed and destructiveness. If everything we do and feel is an expression of God, all moral distinctions are irrelevant. This may seem like a *reductio ad absurdem* of the case, and perhaps it is not so heinous a situation as Westerners, raised on an either–or, good–bad mentality on ethical matters, are apt to judge it; but it remains a stumbling-block for many people. To state that we recognise God throughout the whole of his creation may seem acceptable, even desirable, to those who can sincerely sing of 'all things bright and beautiful', but how heartily can one sing this in the light of 'nature red in tooth and claw', where the stoat kills the rabbit and the ivy stifles the tree? Shelley could write in 'Adonais' of his friend Keats, recently dead:

> He is made one with Nature: there is heard
> His voice in all her music, from the moan
> Of thunder, to the song of night's sweet bird.

And, presumably, in the hiss of the pit viper and the howl of the jackal. Maybe that comment betrays an anthropocentrism which is inappropriate, even impertinent, in pantheistic thought; but what can be said unequivocally is that nature is amoral, so that, inasmuch as it is viewed as a reflection of God's nature, he, too, is amoral. From the pantheist perspective, therefore, all the moral castigations over the ages, made by preachers in God's name, have been a total waste of breath. We shall see the soundness of this outlook as we proceed, specifically in Chapter 10.

One other criticism of pantheism relates to our human sense of initiative and freedom. If all is God, it is asked, what place is there for those qualities which seem (to the enquirer at any rate) integral to her sense of individuality, self-consciousness and autonomy? The resolution of this dilemma (if there is one) must remain until we discuss the mystical experience in Chapter 5.

Animism

Strictly, animism does not belong to any account of differing philosophies of God, but its affinity with some aspects of pantheism justifies a mention here. It derives from the Latin *anima*, meaning 'soul' (the same root as for the word 'animal', which is ironic in view of the fact that the official view of Christianity – to name but one world religion – is that they do not have souls). The primitive view expresses two beliefs. First, all human beings possess, or, perhaps more accurately, are possessed by, souls. These can exist both within and, more significantly, independently of the body. In dreams a person sees the souls of others besides himself appearing as phantoms or eidola – images of their physical appearances. It is also believed that these phantoms have been seen in visions or hallucinations, including phantoms of the dead. It is the absence of the soul which makes all the difference between a corpse and a living being.

By extension, it is believed, at least by some animists, that features of nature also have an anima. A particular rock, or tree, or stream will instil in the onlooker an aura, which he may interpret in terms of the supernatural or holy. Animistic thought is reflected in the Old Testament: in Genesis 28: 22, Jacob dedicates to God the stone on which he has laid his head to sleep with the words, 'This stone which I have set up as a sacred pillar shall be a house of God'. The rock which Moses struck in the wilderness, from which water flowed (Numbers 20: 7–11) may reflect similar thinking. The Christian doctrine of transubstantiation, with its view that the bread and wine become the actual body and blood of Christ, has been described as animistic in its conception, in the sense that physical objects assume a supernatural quality or essence.

Animism was seen by John Le Patourel (from *Chambers Encyclopedia*) as:

> not itself a religion, but a sort of primitive philosophy which controls not only religion but the whole life of the natural man. It represents a stage in the religious evolution which is still represented by the so-called nature-religions, or rather by the poly-daemonistic tribal religions.

Associated with animism is the term *mana*, referring, like animism, to an occult supernatural power which attaches itself to certain sacred objects. Distinctive to the idea of mana is the belief that, being sacred, these objects are therefore *tabu*, which literally means 'not to be lightly approached'. In Melanesia, mana is always connected with some individual who directs it, often wearing on his person a relic of a successful warrior, which gives him the aura he seeks. In other parts of the world the sacred object is described as a fetish. Common to all expressions of animism is the belief in a mystic, quasi-impersonal force which draws from observers a sense of awe and of the supernatural. In the religion of ancient Rome this was described as *numen* and Rudolph Otto, in his *The Idea of the Holy (Das Heilige)*, has developed from this his concept of the numinous, referring to holiness as a state of mind which is brought about by a reaction to the mysterious, the abnormal and the uncanny. His view of religion, which we shall return to in Chapter 5, is a form of religious dread which he describes as *mysterium tremendum* – a mystery giving rise to both fascination and self-abasement. Otto stands in a tradition which is a far cry from that of animism, but I shall be suggesting that his philosophy represents a step, inspired by primitive concepts, towards the acceptance of religion without God. Animism and its cognates may be out of range of what I shall be proposing, but it is not out of bounds.

Theism

Theism expresses the image of God which is the most widely held in the world today, since it is the view taught in the three interconnected world religions which found their earliest expressions in the Middle East: Judaism, Christianity and Islam. The Greek word *theos*, like the Latin *deus*, means God, and the use of two different linguistic sources makes for clarity in designating the differing views. Effectively, theism combines both deism and pantheism, though with its own distinctive gloss. It accepts the transcendental God of the former, but adds the immanent God (gods) of the latter, and the combination gives its believers an image of a God who is both all-powerful and all-loving, terrible in his judgment on the wicked, merciful towards those who truly repent of their sins. The God of theism is thus an intervening God, not the absentee God of deism. It presents the view that, whatever his original intention for the world which he has created, his creatures, consequent to the freedom of choice which he has granted them, have gone astray and so constantly need his counsel and comfort if they are not to be overcome by folly (sin) and despair.

Although today almost all followers of the three religions just mentioned are unlikely to find this a problem, it should be added that, strictly speaking (that is, to be etymologically and, to a lesser extent, historically accurate), the correct word in this context is *monotheism*, where belief in only *one* God is made explicit. So long as we retain the concept of theism as, so far as Judaism, Christianity and Islam are concerned, belief in a supreme being, we are not likely to be confused on this matter.

Two supplementary concepts should be mentioned here. The first is *henotheism*, which reflects a stage between polytheism and monotheism. It acknowledges belief in a supreme being, but one who coexists with other, lesser, divine beings or gods. It is expressed, interestingly enough, in the first of the Ten Commandments: 'You shall have no other gods before me' (Exodus 20: 3). There *are* other gods, but compared with Jehovah they are impotent and worthless. A second view which similarly exemplifies a halfway-house between polytheism and monotheism is *monolatry*, literally only one to worship (Greek *latreia* means worship): again, the existence of other gods is not denied, but, it is affirmed by monolatrists, only their God is *worth* worshipping or, to avoid tautology (since the etymology of both words is the same – *worship* = 'worthship', or 'weorthscipe' in Old English), is *to be* worshipped. Again this is reflected in the Ten Commandments (the second): 'you shall not bow down to them or serve them; for I the Lord your God am a jealous God'.

Dualism (Ditheism)

As the name suggests, this school of thought affirms a belief in two gods, one of whom is normally 'good', the other 'evil', and sees both the history of the world and the battle that occurs within people's souls as arenas for the (inevitable) conflict between the two. It is an attempt to make sense of a world, allegedly created and ruled by a benevolent God, in which evil is continually encountered, whether in human behaviour, or, on a wider canvas, in the 'four horsemen' of the Apocalypse: death, famine, pestilence and war.

The most overtly dualistic of the world's religions is Zoroastrianism, the religion of the followers of the Iranian prophet, Zoroaster (or Zarathustra as it is transliterated from Persian). It is still adhered to by the Guebres of Iran (where they suffer persecution for their beliefs) and the Parsees of India. It expounds the view that the world is governed by a wholly good God, Ahuro Mazda, who is opposed by the evil Angra Mainyu. The Zoroastrian *Gathas* declares:

> Now at the beginning the twin spirits have declared their nature, the better and the evil, in thought and word and deed . . . And when these two spirits came together, in the beginning they established life and non-life.
>
> (Yasna, 30)

Although the ultimate defeat of evil is assured (which is why some Zoroastrian scholars deny that this system of belief is ditheistic), the battle between the two is still proceeding, and followers of this religion are therefore called to commit themselves totally to goodness. It was because of this emphasis on morality that Nietzsche chose the founder of this religion as a focal point of his ground-breaking work *Thus Spake Zarathustra*: he was, Nietzsche believed, the most moral of all the world's religious leaders.

In its attempt to come to terms with the problem of evil in a world allegedly ruled by a benevolent God, theism has not shied away from this expression of dualism. Christianity, for example, has resorted to a personification of evil in the form of Satan, whose power, it teaches, has been dealt a mortal blow through the sacrifice of Jesus the Christ. C. G. Jung (1959) contends that the implication of this belief is that Christianity is ditheistic, since, even if Satan is damned, 'he is *eternal* in his state of damnation'. He adds: 'If Christianity claims to be a monotheism, it becomes unavoidable to assume the opposites as being contained in God.' (The fact is, as has been clear since Hume's famous analysis *Enquiry Concerning the Principles of Morals*, that belief in one supreme God who is both omnipotent and at the same time benevolent founders on the problem of evil. As Hume stated, either God can destroy evil but will not, in which case he is malevolent; or he wants to change things but cannot, in which case he is impotent. Evil is thought of as a 'problem' only because we feel that the situation *ought* to be otherwise: but that is to anticipate later discussion, especially in Chapter 10.)

The Hindu scripture the *Bhagavad-gita* (the key section of the massive *Mahabharata*) illustrates the symbolic nature of dualism. The *Mahabharata* is an account of the battle for the kingdom of Bharata waged between two families, the evil Kauravas and the virtuous Pandavas. Book 6, the *Bhagavad-gita*, contains the instructions before the battle given by the God Krishna to Arjuna, one of the five Pandava brothers. The battle is, in fact, symbolic of the eternal conflict in every individual between the ego and 'higher nature' – or, quite simply, between the good and the bad in everyone. The yin–yang philosophy of China expresses dualism is a different way, suggesting that 'good' and 'bad' cannot exist independently of each other: that we, in fact, can understand the one only in contrast with the other. Consequently, it is false to depict the two as rival forces and, even more harmful, unrealistic to symbolise or personify them as two eternally coexisting rival Gods. Both 'good' and 'evil', as I shall further indicate in Chapter 10, depend on each other to have any meaning at all.

Polytheism

Literally 'many gods', this form of belief has been expressed in numerous societies, both primitive and advanced. The classical world of both the Greeks and the Romans had its pantheons, that is, many gods, each with his or her area of responsibility. Many other civilisations had a similarly wide range of gods and goddesses, for example in Egypt, Mexico, and among the Celts and the Norse. While there is generally a hierarchy among their gods and goddesses, where the highest achieve that status because of the importance of their responsibilities (gods of war are more important than household gods, for instance – perhaps reflecting the male dominance in constructing these pantheons), there is generally no one God who is viewed as being in overall charge.

This is an aspect of polytheism which varies between cultures, however. The Hindus, for example, express belief in many gods, such as Rama, Vishnu, Shiva and his consort Kali, but Brahman is held to be the ultimate source of all that exists. In some communities the idea is held that while there is one supreme God who retains ultimate responsibility for the world and its happenings, he has delegated his authority to divine functionaries who work as directed by, and are responsible to, him. Maybe, as Geoffrey Parrinder suggests (*Religion in an African City*), we need 'to devise a term which would denote religions that have a supreme God and also worship other gods'. Many expressions of polytheism fall into this category since, as William James suggests (1960, p. 141), it has 'shown itself well satisfied with a universe composed of many original principles, provided we be allowed to believe that the divine principle remains supreme, and that others are subordinate'.

Panentheism

This is the doctrine that, while God is manifested in all living creatures, as pantheists believe, that is not the whole story: if it were, it would imply that God exists only so long as Nature exists; so when, as is inevitable eventually, the world comes to an end, he will die with it. The word means 'all-in-God' and was rescued from obscurity by John Robinson in his sequel to *Honest to God*, *Explorations into God*. He argued that the panentheistic view, in a way not always found in theism, made explicit apropos of God that he was both immanent and transcendent, present in all living things but not dependent on their existence for his own: he is omnipresent and eternal throughout the universe and, if need be, beyond. Add to this the interventionist theology of theism, and, Robinson suggested, we have the most philosophically satisfying view of God's being, and of his relationship both with the universe in general and all forms of life, human or otherwise, in particular.

These, then, are some of the major delineations of God, or gods, which have found acceptance among human beings since the earliest historical times. The list is not totally comprehensive, but I hope that enough categories have been included to embrace the ideas of most people who affirm a belief in the deity. Two issues remain to be reflected upon before turning to the question of *why* people have come to any of these beliefs.

A classification of types

From the amalgam just presented, I think it is possible to classify the various expressions of belief under three main headings. The first, and most primitive, is the polytheistic and animistic set of beliefs. While sometimes expressing the idea of one supreme being who delegates some of his powers to subordinates, the more general picture is of a large number of deities, each with a particular area of responsibility. Some areas are more extensive, and the gods responsible for them consequently more 'important', than others, but the general scene is one of a cabinet (with perhaps a *primus inter pares*), and not a dictatorship.

The second category is monotheism. Where this is the belief, it is held that there is one God only who has revealed his power through the original creation of the universe and apart from in classical deism, continues to reveal himself throughout the world in his role as guide and guardian of the people whom he has created. It is to him that they are continuously, and will be ultimately, answerable.

The third type is more difficult to name, since it contains facets of most of the categories mentioned earlier. It includes elements of pantheism, especially in its emphasis on the harmony of an individual with the natural world, the unavoidable context of his living, and on the sense of the divine which runs through him. Otto's conception of the numinous is close to what I am implying. Perhaps the most convenient word is mysticism, and we shall remain with that for the present, recognising, as will be outlined later, that we need to give it a connotation and context which broadens it out from its traditional usage.

Most of the world's religions have elements of all three types in their belief systems, though normally one is dominant. The religion which affirms all three without making a value judgment about their respective merits is Hinduism. This religion will be discussed in some detail in Chapter 6, but it is worth noting here that the Hindu scriptures – the Vedas, with the Upanishads, the *Mahabharata*, with the *Bhagavad-gita*, the *Ramayana* and so on – include all three types. Sometimes they express a belief in many gods – Brahman, Vishnu, Krishna, Shiva and numerous others; at other times a belief in one absolute God, Brahman; and elsewhere a belief in the mystical experience as the ultimate reality, the discovery of the oneness of the individual Atman with the Brahman, the ground of being – a discovery which means entry into the state of moksha, enlightenment, where one can say with total certainty, 'tat tvam asi': thou art (or I am) that.

I shall be arguing that it is along this path that we need to tread if we are to experience religion which is unencumbered either by ancient mythology or modern pseudo-psychology; here faith is replaced with experience and knowledge. But the path is wider than that to which even Hinduism, the most religious of the world's religions, bears witness.

Attributes of God

Monotheists declare that God is perfect, and this concept is the basis, as we shall see, of the ontological argument for his existence. 'Perfect' sounds a straightforward-enough term, but what it means exactly becomes more difficult to determine the more closely it is examined. It can be used casually, of course, as when we describe someone as a perfect fool, or as looking like a perfect angel, but in this usage the epithet adds little to the name; we may have a perfect copy of a document, in the sense that it is an exact replica of the original, but would we be justified in describing a copy of a famous painting as 'a perfect forgery'? Generally, we use the term to mean 'that which cannot be improved on' which, so far as human beings and their inventions and creations are concerned, is impossible. There is, for instance, no such thing as a perfectly tuned motor engine: with more sophisticated equipment we should be able to increase, however infinitessimally, its accuracy; similarly, there is no such person as a perfect lady or gentleman, no perfect body or perfect mind. Similarly, there is nobody who is morally perfect. Even assuming that we could reach a consensus about what the word 'good' means in reference to a human character, which is expecting the impossible since we are dealing with an evaluative term about whose meaning there will always be wide-ranging disagreement (as will be further discussed in Chapter 10), it is inconceivable that everyone everywhere would agree that any particular person had attained such a standard of goodness that he or she could not be better. Yet the New Testament calls for this quality: 'You must be perfect, as your heavenly father is perfect' (Matt 5: 48).

The attributes of God which theologians and philosophers of religion (who do not always belong to the same stable, of course) have extrapolated over the centuries to categorise his perfection will be readily agreed on. God is:

- almighty (omnipotent in the latinised version of the word): he *can do anything*;
- all-knowing (omniscient): he *knows everything*;
- all-present (omnipresent): he *is everywhere*;
- everlasting (eternal): he *is without beginning or end*;

(these last two characteristics are contained in the word universal, often ascribed to God)

- unchangeable (immutable): he *is forever the same*;
- limitless (infinite): a word which embraces several of the foregoing designations, meaning that he is *inexhaustible*, and illustrated in the hymn 'O God thou bottomless abyss'.

The trouble with this list is that though the qualities referred to spring readily to people's lips when talking of God's perfection, it is beyond the mind of man to picture what any of them means in actuality. If, for instance, God is almighty, does that mean he can do anything he decides to do, even act against logic by arranging that every other day a triangle can have four sides, or that on the Sabbath an object can both exist and not exist at the same time, breaking the Law of Contradiction? If he cannot achieve these, does that mean that his almightiness is bound by the rules of logic? A monotheist may well argue that, since God created the rules, and since he is unchangeable, he is simply abiding by what he himself established. But if that is the case, does it not suggest that his immutability is inconsistent with his omnipotence? The monotheist might reply that what is not broken doesn't need mending – and that the laws of logic fit into this category. (The scriptural fundamentalist has, of course, no problem with logic: he can, for instance, cheerfully accept the two contradictory accounts of the creation contained in Genesis 1 and 2, with the defence that these differences simply illustrate St Paul's affirmation that 'the foolishness of God is wiser than men'. Thus do some people break the first commandment, which includes loving God with all the mind.)

Karen Armstrong (op. cit.) has shown in her comprehensive survey that, whether or not God is himself immutable, his image over the centuries and in different cultures has certainly changed. The monotheist may defend his position by affirming that, while human understanding of him may have changed, he has been always the same – waiting, it may be presumed, to be fully discovered and understood. If this is the case, it follows that any statements about God, like those made about the physical world (as Popper has indicated) can be seen as no more than provisional, however certain they may seem from our current perspective.

Perhaps the monotheist will eventually be able to resolve the dilemma created by another of God's attributes – his omniscience. If God knows everything, this knowledge must be of the future as well as the past (and the present, if there is such a thing: time, after all, is the continuous process of the 'not yet' moving inexorably into the 'no longer'). If he knows only what has happened up to now (which, as I write, is already in the past), then he knows no more than what can be known by a *very* knowledgeable scholar – or, at any rate, a group of scholars – who, or most of whom, would hardly wish to claim to be gods. Yet if God knows the future, this implies that he knows all that is to become of us. What price, then, freewill, autonomy and personal initiative?

The situation here is bristling with problems, which are hardly eased by the attribution of human qualities to the infinite being: a process of *anthropomorphism*, meaning 'in the form of man'. These qualities describe God in terms which are more readily accessible to mortal beings because we encounter them among our fellows on a daily basis. Thus God is proclaimed as one who loves his creatures, cares for them, guides them when they are perplexed, comforts them in times of sorrow, strengthens them in times of trial, forgives them their sins and, if all goes well, finally rewards them with an eternal place in his presence. There is also another side to his nature, equally expressive of human qualities. He can be jealous, wrathful, destructive, vengeful and, ultimately, condemnatory as he sits in judgment on his creatures. Armstrong illustrates from theistic sources how the latter qualities were gradually replaced by the former in the minds of the authors of those scriptures; but the anthropomorphism remains: God possesses human qualities to the highest conceivable extent, all, in short, perfectly expressed. He is the ideal father, the most considerate lover, the wisest advocate and the most unbiased judge.

The problem with these anthropomorphic characterisations, as opposed to the more philosophical terms used earlier, is that they have the effect of bringing God down to human level, and depend for their effectiveness on what, for human beings, always requires physical organisms. Thus God is (almost) always male; he is the father of his people, the bridegroom to his faithful worshippers. It may be argued that if we called God 'she' we would have the same anthropomorphic problem, which is intensified if we call him 'it'. (To affirm that we need a new pronoun which means 'he and/or she and/or it' simply begs the question raised in this book: why speak of God at all? – but we will hold that topic over until Chapter 5.) At this stage of the enquiry, it is enough to be aware that any kind of talk about God, who is perfect, is bound to be expressed inadequately, and that what words we use are the best we can manage after many generations of reflection on the matter. To realise that all God-talk is inadequate is to recognise a situation very little different from that of a musician attempting to characterise the inspiration behind his compositions, or a poet describing his muse.

The philosopher Ludwig Feuerbach (1804–72) argued that God, as an image held in people's minds, was nothing more than a product of anthropomorphism. In his most famous book *Das Wesen des Christentums*, translated by George Eliot as *The Essence of Christianity*, he described religion as 'the dream of the human mind', arguing that human beings project their own ideals and natures on to an illusory God. God was thus the personification of the best thinking of which the human mind was capable, with a character which epitomised the best behaviour which they could engage in and the noblest principles which they could follow. For Feuerbach, theology was concerned with the nature of man rather than God: man was, he argued, the only true *ens realissimum*, or most real being ('ens' is the present participle of the Latin 'esse', to be, and 'realissimum' the superlative of the adjective 'reale', which is self-explicatory).

Process theology

A view on the nature of God which was first expounded a century ago, but has yet to be accommodated into theistic teaching, is process theology. It was first openly discussed by the philosopher A. N. Whitehead (1861–1947), but was given a wider public through the writings of Pierre Teilhard De Chardin (1881–1955), especially in his book *The Phenomenon of Man*, which, initially refused an imprimatur by the Roman Catholic Church, was eventually published in 1959 after his death, publication having been refused despite the fact that he was a Jesuit priest, but perhaps because he was also a palaeontologist. It is significant that the introduction to this book was written by the humanist, Julian Huxley.

Process theology teaches that God cannot be understood in the theistic tradition alone, but only if to this tradition are added the main developments in science, especially the science of evolution. God's way of working in the world is a slow process, so that we are given a picture of him working to overcome the evil that is present in the universe, together with the element of chance, or accident, which it contains.

God is thus viewed as one who is not so much self-sufficient as involved in the long, patience-demanding process of bringing about what Teilhard termed the *noosphere*, a state beyond the biosphere, where the mind is the supremely active agent of events. This idiosyncratic representation of God's immanence almost reaches the point of declaring that he is not omnipotent, because he cannot do what he wants where and when he wants, but must work alongside his creation to bring about the new higher state: a process which seems to imply that God is also not unchangeable, as earlier described. This theology has appealed to numerous modern theologians and philosophers of religion; but it, like earlier views, still remains fixed on the view of God's necessity, which is precisely the issue under discussion. It is time to turn our attention to the question of why this point of view has such a hold on *Homo sapiens*.

Chapter 4

Why God?

A man with God is always in the majority

(John Knox)

There are certain statements about belief in God which are, I think, beyond doubt. First, the majority of the human race hold this belief; which is to say that, viewed from the opposite angle, only a minority of the human race are atheists. Second, if asked to explain what they mean by God, we should have a cornucopia of replies, some similar to one another, some at variance with others, some totally inconsistent with each other. Third, a fair proportion of those professing this belief would find it difficult to say anything worthwhile about it except that they prefer to think of the world as in some way under the control of an almighty being rather than as one which is left to fend for itself; these millions – billions? – thus constitute the silent majority who will, if it comes to the crunch, vote for God against any non-theistic alternative.

What we must now explore is why this is the case: why, in a world which increasingly rejoices in the fruits of scientific and medical discoveries and the technological developments to which these give birth, God endures; why, when men and women are called to take more responsibility for themselves, they still feel the need for a divine guiding hand; why, in short, reports on God's death seem, like the similar report sent to the Associated Press apropos of Mark Twain, to be greatly exaggerated.

The catalyst for belief in God, analogous to either a rock or quicksand according to one's perspective, is the human desire for a sense of order and purpose in their lives and, by extension, in the world around them. Chaos, chance, accident are all the bridesmaids of aimlessness, anarchy, nihilism. Even though they cannot perceive it themselves, multitudes of people pay lip service to a master plan for the universe, a scheme which would, if they were able to grasp it, make sense of the confusion, the disorder, what Camus termed the *absurd*, to which their path through life constantly

testifies. Like children reading a fairy tale, they want a happy-ever-after conclusion to the struggle; they want to be able to say with R. L. Stevenson, 'I
believe in the ultimate goodness of things; and if I awoke in hell I should
still believe it.'

What they don't seem able to come to terms with is a view on life like that
expressed in a famous (and mellifluous) passage by Bertrand Russell:

> That Man is the product of causes which had no preview of the end they
> were achieving; that his origin, his growth, his hopes and fears, his loves
> and his beliefs, are but the outcome of accidental collocations of atoms;
> that no fire, no heroism, no intensity of thought and feeling, can preserve
> an individual life beyond the grave; that all the labours of the ages, all
> the devotion, all the inspiration, all the noonday brightness of human
> genius, are destined to extinction in the vast death of the solar system,
> and that the whole temple of Man's achievement must inevitably be
> buried beneath the debris of a universe in ruins – all these things, if not
> quite beyond dispute, are yet so nearly certain, that no philosophy which
> rejects them can hope to stand. Only within the scaffolding of these
> truths, only on the firm foundation of unyielding despair, can the soul's
> habitation henceforth be safely built.
>
> (*Mysticism and Logic*)

Even acknowledging that Russell has – as was not uncommon in his quasi-
mischievous anti-Christian writings – allowed his gift for colourful
expression to lead him to hyperbolise the message (especially the final sentence which seems overdrawn, an example of what Kahlil Gibran termed 'a
truth that has lost its temper'), the nihilistic attitude implied in the passage
is not exclusive to Russell, and a fair proportion of the human race find it
threatening, disturbing, even repellant. If there is no ultimate meaning in anything, even in those aspects of the human condition in which they can take
pride, why do we continue to care? If, *pace* the dying Hamlet, 'the rest is
silence', why the preliminary sounds? If all our strivings can be summed up
in the legend on a Hindu gravestone: 'I was not; I was miserable; I am not' –
then why the slot in the middle? So the quest for a Holy Grail, a golden
thread – in a word, God – occupies, even if only subliminally, the minds of
countless representatives of the human race. At times of deep national or
personal crisis such thinking is likely to surface, as the many who spend most
of their lives without overt reference to God join those who defer to him continually.

So we find that God has been seized upon as the concept *par excellence*
with which people have faced down the view which they found unbearable:
that the world is dominated by accident, purposelessness, or what Dryden
termed 'the various turns of chance'. We must now examine in some detail
the main areas which, throughout history, have called for this palliative,

whether to give relief to the intellectual anguish of uncertainty, or to lessen the pain brought on by unfortunate physical or emotional circumstances.

'Proofs' of God's existence: the God of the gaps

The philosophical arguments for God's existence will be familiar to any student of metaphysics, and can therefore merit only a brief rehearsal here. In the process, two considerations should be borne in mind. First, the strength of the arguments lies in the extent to which they make intelligible certain problems which, at the time when the arguments were first presented, seemed to leave a huge logical and/or situational lacuna if the concept of God were not introduced. Second, and integrally linked to this issue, lacunae of this magnitude fell foul of the natural desire, outlined above, to find meaning in the universe, so that it seemed to be going against nature when faced with apparently insuperable problems like that of suffering, or of evil, the mysteries of time and eternity, and above all, of accident and chance, to give a shrug of the shoulders and get on with the ironing. It offered relief amid the insecurity integral to this situation to seize on an answer which, by filling the gaps (lacunae), provided safe ground to tread on.

The cosmological argument

This argument posits the existence of God from the existence of the world. It combines the first four of Thomas Aquinas's *Quinque viae* (Five Ways, or Paths) in his *Summa theologica*. The argument, which, like much of Aquinas' teaching, goes back to Aristotle, is based on the principle of causality. We observe that everything that exists or happens has a cause: the stone that falls, the tree that grows, the door that opens were all caused by some preceding event such as the kicking (by someone) of the stone, the sun which warmed and the rain which watered the ground in which the tree grew, the draught which blew on the door. By extension, the same principle applies on the infinitely wider stage of the universe. Whether it began as a void or as the original black hole, something must have caused the explosion which led to the existence of the myriads of spheres of which it is constituted: if *nothing* caused this to happen, then the original argument, that everything which happens has a cause, is false. Since we have nothing tangible to fall back on as the cause of the universe, the proponents of this argument simply ascribe it to God, of whom St Anselm was to state: 'There never was a time when he was not, and there never will be a time when he will not be.' (Interestingly, exactly the same statement, except that the first person is used instead of the third, is made by the god Krishna to Arjuna before the battle as recounted in the *Bhagavad-gita* (see p. 24), written 2,000 years before Anselm arrived.)

It is immediately obvious that this attempt to avoid breaking the law of causality has been hoist with its own petard: the obvious reply is to ask who made God. To describe him as 'the uncaused first cause' refutes the principle on which the argument is based; and to declare that God, being a spirit, is therefore not subject to the laws of matter, simply increases the confusion. As Immanuel Kant argued, if God does not belong to the world of phenomena, but is a reality beyond them, then they must both be totally independent of each other. Modern explorations into acausality which are being pursued in the field of quantum physics – explorations which advance David Hume's examination of causality two centuries ago – also serve to weaken this 'proof'.

The fact is that, granted our finite minds, any statement about the origin of the universe is beyond any form of thought, as examples will illustrate. I may say:

1   There was nothing, and out of nothing the universe came into being. But nothing can come from nothing.
2   There was nothing, and out of nothing God came into being, and eventually created the universe. Same comment.
3   Matter, whether as a black hole or in some earlier form, has always been in existence: it never had a beginning, so there is no need for the cosmological argument. But if it never had a beginning, how did we reach the present moment in time?
4   God has always existed and, whether 6,000 years ago (as Archbishop Ussher stated in his marginal dates to the bible) or six billion years ago (as modern astrophysicists are suggesting), created the universe. Same comment as for 3.

All four statements illustrate the fact that the human mind, created in time and viewing everything that happens as having a beginning, a middle and an end, cannot comprehend the concept of eternity, or the equally impossible concept of time as having begun at a certain moment before which there was 'no time'.

None the less, those who cling to the cosmological argument are happy to acknowledge the logical difficulties but fall back on the comforting view that, in St Paul's words quoted earlier, 'The foolishness of God is wiser than men' (I Cor. 1: 25). For those who take refuge in this stance, it is enough to accept the idea of God as an explanation of the cosmos, without pursuing the matter any further. They are, as Schopenhauer remarked, like people who take a taxi to a chosen destination and, having alighted from it, lose all interest in its subsequent journeys. For many of them, however, the cosmological argument is linked with a second 'proof', which we must now consider.

The argument from design: the teleological argument

If the cosmological argument concerns itself with the first cause, the teleological argument relates to a final cause, ('telos' means end, purpose, design or plan). In the eighteenth century it was known as the 'physico-theological' argument, and it springs from the fact that, as we observe them, each species has precisely the number of organs, cells and so on in order to fulfil itself and serve its own needs. This argument is strengthened rather than weakened by the knowledge of evolution which has grown during the past two centuries, since evolution teaches that the ultimate aim of all creatures is to survive, and this they evidently have accomplished; and, teleologists aver, the link between evolution and teleology is not weakened by the fact that many species have, over the millennia, become extinct: they, because of circumstances alien to their survival, simply failed to fulfil that purpose.

Applied to the human context, the argument extends to people's belief in a goal in life, a golden thread running through it which enables them to make some kind of sense of what otherwise may seem no more than a treadmill. This may not quite be what Tennyson meant when he wrote of 'that one far-off divine event/ To which the whole creation moves', but it represents a similar conviction that, in stark contradistinction to Russell's sentiments quoted earlier, there is a master plan for the universe established by God, the first cause; and everything we do, every decision we make, can be part of that plan, so that even the apparently trivial pursuits of daily life assume a meaning and purpose which gives them an eternal dimension.

So far as the teleological argument is concerned, this latter consideration is strictly beside the point. From the teleological perspective, the evidence reveals design in the universe; design implies that there was a plan; and a plan requires a planner. But another interpretation of the phenomena which some see as the hand of God at work, calls for a different approach to evolution from that discussed above. From this perspective, the creative process had nothing to do with a pre-existent master plan, but was simply a matter of (in Spencer's words) 'the survival of the fittest'. That is to say, those species prospered which, fortuitously, had characteristics which increased their chances of survival – long enough, at any rate, to enable them to reproduce their kind and pass on their genes to the next generation. Those not so fortunate ceased to exist, a fate suffered by countless numbers of species, which incidentally implies that if God, the master planner, was in charge, he made the kind of mistakes which are hardly consonant with omniscience.

Thus we have an objection based on logic. If God is, by definition, perfect, it follows that everything he does, everything he creates, must be perfect. If this were not the case, how otherwise are we to conclude that he is 'that than which no better can be conceived'? To say something like 'of course, anyone can see that the universe is full of imperfections, but I still know that God is perfect' would make as much sense as saying that though a particular tennis player loses as many matches as he wins, he is still the best player imaginable. God's perfection – his omnipotence, omniscience and so on – must be manifest through the evidence of his works, *not in spite of them*.

The concept of teleology is sometimes identified in history. It is argued that the golden thread mentioned earlier runs through human affairs, directing historical events towards a divinely ordained goal: but such a view seems to reflect make-believe rather than reality. We are all still directed, one could say determined, by our basic drives such as aggression, reproduction, the territorial and tribal instincts. The way in which these are expressed, and the terrain in which they manifest themselves, may have changed with changing social patterns but their strength, for better or for worse, is undiminished. Tribal and national wars persist on the planet; murders occur round the clock, half of them caused by sexual jealousy; and in societies which are becoming increasingly multiracial, overt expressions of venom are made regularly by members of one race towards another. If there is a golden thread, it seems to be shaped more like a figure-of-eight than a straight line. The single example of the holocaust, perpetrated by one of the most civilised nations on earth, should lead us to acknowledge that the golden thread is a mirage, the theory of progress a pipe dream, and its upholders living on fantasy island. H. A. L. Fisher's laconic comment in his *History of Europe* seems apposite: while some may identify progress in history, such insight had been denied to him. The renaissance of national socialism in the twenty-first century in parts of Europe, which one would expect to be most repelled by it, suggests that there is no continuity in history, but that every generation must learn afresh from its own mistakes. As Hegel wrote in his *Philosophy of History*:

> What experience and history teach is this – that people and governments never have learned anything from history, or acted on principles deduced from it.

Rather than identifying a golden thread, we would surely be wiser to accept the definition of history offered in Bierce's *The Devil's Dictionary*: 'a story, mostly false, of events, mostly unimportant, conducted by rulers, mostly knaves, and soldiers, mostly fools.'

The ontological argument

This famous argument, associated with René Descartes (1596–1650) and St Anselm (1033–1109), attempts to prove that God is logically necessary. 'Ontos' is the present participle of the Greek verb 'to be', so the argument concerns the understanding of being. Immanuel Kant averred in his *Critique of Pure Reason* that this proof was effectively the basis of the other two classical proofs already discussed:

> Thus the physico-theological proof of the existence of an original or supreme being rests upon the cosmological proof, and the cosmological upon the ontological.

It is, at the same time, both the most philosophically satisfying of all the arguments and the most tautological. Any reader who is contemplating entering the Roman Catholic priesthood (which, at the moment, excludes the female half, but times and attitudes may change) can expect to spend many seminars studying its complexities. It is based on the concept of a being who cannot be improved on, as defined on p. 27. In Latin the statement reads, 'Aliquid quo nihil maiorum cogitare est.' If, so the argument goes, this perfect being (A) does not in fact exist, it would then be theoretically possible for another being (B) to exist who has all the attributes of being (A) – but with the crucial extra feature of existence. We then, however, place ourselves in a logical impasse, since we began by describing being (A) as perfect, and are now hypothesising about being (B) who has perfection *plus* (existence). It is impossible to be more perfect than perfect, and, anyway, nothing could be described as perfect if it doesn't even exist. Existence must, then, be a facet of God's perfection. Therefore God (being (A)) exists.

Satisfying though this argument may seem (and has seemed to many who have thought it through over the past millennium) there are three counter-arguments to it. First, as the monk Gaunilo pointed out in his attack on St Anselm's exposition of the argument in *Proslogium*, one might just as well assert that because I have in my mind an image of a perfect island, with an agreeable climate and life-sustaining plants and crops, it must exist, because otherwise it would be possible for another island to exist which really had these qualities. In other words, nothing can be *defined* into existence. The defender of the argument will reply that the existence of God is a different form of thought than that of an island, or a house, or a cat: their existence is not necessary for their perfection; God's existence, as the ontological argument makes clear, is essential to it. As F. J. Copleston states in his *History of Philosophy*:

> If God is possible, i.e. if the idea of the all-perfect and necessary Being contains no contradiction, God must exist, since it would be absurd to speak of a *merely possible necessary Being* (it is a contradiction in terms), whereas there is no contradiction in speaking of merely possible beautiful islands.
>
> (Vol. II, p. 163)

Copleston's defence of the argument serves only to invite the second objection, which Kant discussed at length in his *Critique*: existence is not a property of anything: that is to say, it is unnecessary to add this feature when giving a list of a thing's, or a creature's, characteristics. If I say that a giraffe has four long legs, a tail, a long neck, and so on, it is not relevant to add 'and it exists', since that is implied in the description of its properties; with that final phrase we are making a separate statement, which is precisely the point at issue. It is fair to state that *if* there is a greatest conceivable being, then this being exists; but we are still left high and dry about whether there *is* in fact a greatest conceivable being.

The third counter-argument concerns the nature of ontology – what we mean by 'to be', which is a highly complex matter, as readers of Heidegger's *Being and Time* will testify. At its most elemental, any discussion in this field must include a crucial issue which the ontological argument for God's existence, as outlined above, ignores: the difference between 'to be' and 'to exist'. Ask my grandson James whether there are such creatures as unicorns and he will happily draw one; but to ask if unicorns exist is to enter a different form of thought. It is a difference which the German language draws out in distinguishing between 'es ist' and 'es gibt' – 'there is' and 'there exists'. The example given to beginners in the German language is 'Es ist ein Mann im Monde; es gibt aber keinen Mann im Monde': 'There is a man-in-the-moon; but no man in the moon exists (or no man exists in the moon).' So it can be argued that there is a supreme being because many people hold him in mind, obey him, worship him; but it does not follow that this supreme being exists. They could all be either deluding themselves or, as I shall suggest later, misinterpreting their experiences.

The moral argument

This argument was first introduced by Immanuel Kant as he attempted to prove that, while he had (to his own satisfaction) demolished the three arguments already considered, God must exist, since there was no other way to explain why we feel a moral compulsion to behave in certain ways. He had suggested three stages whereby a secure and universal moral guideline could be identified. First, he affirmed (uncontentiously) that the greatest human quality is goodwill – empathy, compassion, benevolence and so on. But these are evaluative, even vague, terms which need to be given identifiable expression: how can we be sure that what we do is actually motivated by goodwill? How can we avoid self-deception? He answered that the sure guide was the sense of *duty*: obey that, and we can be confident of avoiding self-interest disguised as charity, of making a virtue of what we desire in any case. This leads to his final consideration: how can anyone be certain where his duty lies? Kant's answer was his categorical imperative – to act only on the maxim that whatever one considers doing could be made a universal law. In other words, when faced with a moral dilemma involving either course (C) or course (D), a person should reflect on whether he would prefer a world in which everyone followed (C) or one in which everyone followed (D). Having decided that, he has resolved the dilemma and his duty is clear.

What remained unresolved, however, was the question of what it was that gave the moral agent the confidence that course (C), say, was the right way to follow: for example, that, if finding a lost purse, it should be returned to its original owner and not simply pocketed. But how can one be certain that this imperative was right and any other wrong? To answer that it is known intuitively is simply to remove the problem a further stage back. Why does the intuition point in one direction rather than another?

Kant's answer was that it must be because God, who is not so much a moral God as the essence or personification of morality, has established the right course as an act of his will. He must therefore exist, since otherwise there is no satisfactory answer to the question of the source of our sense of what is morally right. (Similarly, Kant suggested, there must be a heaven, since otherwise those who follow the right path yet still suffer, and those who take the wrong path yet prosper, would not be receiving their just deserts. Heaven would take care of that anomaly.)

We shall be discussing later the future of morality without God, so two brief comments are all that are required here. The first is that Kant's argument is a clear case of using God as a *deus ex machina*: his argument is left in a state of suspension without this final touch, just as the story of Little Red Riding Hood is horrific without the introduction of the woodcutter at the end; what must be faced is the possibility that the theory is either wrong or needs to be modified. The second comment concerns a viewpoint which arose as man's evolutionary development became more widely understood: over the centuries, people have discovered that certain forms of behaviour 'work' and others do not. By 'working' is meant that they are more likely to bring groups together, thus enabling them to be more united – and therefore more equipped to overcome any enemies intent on destroying them. To take Kant's own example, goodwill is better than malevolence because it is more likely to enable those communities who practise it to survive. Thus trial and error over many millennia, not an omnipotent being, has brought about the sense that some forms of behaviour should be encouraged, others discouraged, sometimes on pain of death. It is significant that all the world's moral codes agree in banning killing, stealing, lying and certain sexual practices because these activities are all likely to lead to disunity in the tribe or group which condones them.

These four arguments are known as the 'proofs' of God's existence. What must not be lost sight of is that they are all human constructs, the product of human need: in this case, the need to feel that one does not have to lay aside rationality or logic in order to believe in God, but, on the contrary, rest assured that reason and revelation, sanity and sanctity, complement one another. The case is not proven, of course, because rationality can just as viably lead to atheism; but at least the case for God is given a certain academic respectability through these 'proofs'.

These classical arguments have all been presented by men with outstanding minds and total integrity. However, there are two inherent weaknesses in the case so far which need a mention before considering the issue from a different angle. The first is that the arguments *are* human constructs: they gave renown to those who first constructed them, but whether they actually lead to a clearer understanding of God or not is another matter, since it is doubtful if anyone ever came to believe in him by the process they follow. In fact, the devout Jew Martin Buber argued in his *I and Thou* that they were a hindrance to true belief, exalting the human quality of intelligence at the expense of a genuine religious experience. Furthermore, they remain a defence of the God 'out there' (to quote the phrase used with great effect by John Robinson in his *Honest to God*). None of them, with the possible exception of the moral argument, makes of him a God in the midst, immanent rather than transcendent (and even the moral argument uses the idea of a God 'out there' to resolve a problem in the midst). According to the terms used so far, God is no more than a theory; and, significantly, one which can be appreciated only by those with sufficient mental skills to follow the intricacies of the argument. Manifestly, a great proportion of those who have in the past expressed confidence in his existence, together with many contemporary believers in him, have been and are untouched by this *modus operandi*, and we must now examine the paths that have led them to believe.

As with the philosophical arguments, based on the conviction that there *must* be a resolution to intellectual dilemmas (otherwise uncertainty and ignorance rule), so with the more practical considerations which follow: *Homo sapiens* finds it difficult to come to terms with a world at the mercy of chance, or accept that things happen just because they happen. The question 'why?' surfaces continually, and the answer has to be one which gives the questioner a sense of well-being and security.

God as the answer to human inadequacies

The circumstance which is the catalyst of the examples which follow is the inability of *Homo sapiens* to control certain situations. Some relate mainly to earlier times, but some remain as challenging (or almost) as they ever were.

The need for seasonal weather was a major concern in earliest agrarian times when the health, if not actual survival, of a tribe or local community depended to a great extent on seasonal rains and sunshine. Since the weather in many parts of the globe is notoriously fickle, and since people did not have the sense of security to allow that it was all a matter of the luck of the draw, they fell back on the idea of a God who knew what he was about, but was somewhat canny in revealing his plan to his creatures. The people's task was then to discover what he required in order to ensure that he would meet their climatic needs. In many early communities this sense led to the introduction of rites and rituals, particularly at seedtime and harvest, which were believed to be pleasing to God. Even today, with our advanced technology, on Rogation Sunday (in the spring) there is a ceremony in many rural areas for the blessing of the fields, with the invocation of God's providence so as to make them fertile; and large numbers of scientifically trained people are happy to sing at harvest time,

> We plough the fields, and scatter
> The good seed on the land;
> But it is fed and watered
> By God's almighty hand . . .

and bring into the church their 'first fruits', so echoing promises made to God in earliest times to encourage him, in turn, to be true to his original promise that 'seed time and harvest shall not cease upon the earth' (Genesis 8: 22). With the advent of modern technology and international trade this need is for most people less strident than it was, but traces or echos of it remain in twenty-first-century communities.

Sickness and disease occupy another area of human inadequacy. Why do people become ill? More to the point, why do some contract a particular disease and others, for no apparent reason and with no markedly different lifestyles, avoid it? Today we know of the human genome, of social conditions, of early diets and unhealthy habits, all of which play a part in causing or preventing disease, but it still remains a mystery why some suffer more than others. Most people today will call for the doctor when they are ill, rather than a witch doctor or priest, but any priest can expect to spend a fair amount of his time visiting the sick and praying with them for their recovery; and no act of worship is without such prayers.

Here again is an expression of the desire to identify a purpose, a meaning, in all that happens. Sickness happens, therefore it must be part of God's intention for his creatures: perhaps to test their faith or fortitude, to create in them an empathy with other suffering creatures, to punish them for past misdeeds, or to remind them that they, not being omniscient like him, have only a limited overview of the human situation. Whatever the reason for disease may be, God knows what he is doing; so his creatures must accept on trust that all, by whatever circuitous and devious paths, will ultimately be well. These are some of the arguments introduced in the face of the manifest evil in a world allegedly created by a benevolent God. It is part of 'the problem of evil', and we shall return to it later. At this stage it need only be said that while ignorance about the indeterminate situation remained, it was outweighed by the confidence that God had the matter in hand. Terra firma had been struck.

Natural disasters, particularly when violent phenomena occur, have always been a reminder of human impotence. We may have come to terms with thunder-and-lightning storms (though the author has seen all the employees of a hotel in Naples down tools and flee to a next-door chapel during one such: we were not served dinner that evening), but the occurrence of floods, hurricanes, earthquakes, volcanic eruptions, droughts and famines can bring even the most advanced of civilisations to its knees, both metaphorically and literally: in 1977, for instance, after weeks of drought, a national day of prayer for rain was called in the UK, showing that, however sophisticated they might claim to be, *in extremis* many still return to the concept of purposiveness behind every event. Others have had no compunction in describing the spread of AIDS as God's judgment on homosexuals which, according to Leviticus 18: 22, he had condemned as 'an abomination'. Had the same people been around in 1755, they may well have described the earthquake which destroyed the centre of Lisbon as God's judgment on Roman Catholicism – especially as, being a Sunday, most of those who perished were at church when it happened, as Voltaire regularly reminded his theistic critics. Albert Einstein spoke for all who seek out God's providence when left defenceless and insecure by natural catastrophes, with his affirmation, 'God does not play dice'.

A further area of insecurity is where *births* are concerned. It is only in relatively recent times that parents have had any real control over the number of offspring they bring into the world. Take up any novel written a century ago, and the reader is likely to find a phrase like, 'God blessed our marriage with *x* number of children'. Where new life was concerned, God's creative power had to be acknowledged. Today, we ourselves (or most of us) assume responsibility for the number of offspring that we bring into the world; but the older attitude remains the official view of the largest denomination in Christendom, the Roman Catholic Church, who claim to number as its members about a tenth of the world's population. The use of any kind of artificial form of birth control is, as a Papal Encyclical of 1996 defined it, 'intrinsically evil': that is, it is evil even if every human being on earth apart from the Pope thinks otherwise. In Europe this offensive and myopic statement is largely ignored: the lowest birth-rate in the world is in fact in Italy, the home of the Vatican; but the spread of AIDS among African and South American communities who have listened and obeyed has led some to call for the arraignment of the Pope on a charge of genocide (the *Guardian*, *c.* early 2000). Here is an issue where the alleged will and purpose of God is alien to that of the people. It is becoming a catalyst of change in people's attitudes to an almighty, omniscient being: either he changes his mind, or we will change ours about him. It seems that the writing is on the wall, and the penmanship is that of those, growing daily in number, who, in John Robinson's words (op. cit.), have 'come of age'.

Death remains for some 'the last enemy' (I Cor. 15: 26); for all, the greatest mystery. More than any other feature of our existence, it creates the need for God. It is the knowledge of our finitude – a knowledge unique to *Homo sapiens* – that creates the anxiety, the fear of non-existence which, in turn, is the catalyst of the idea of an infinite being with whom, or through whom, his creatures might live forever. Death is the supreme motivator so far as belief in God is concerned. (A positive point for non-believers to bear in mind, however, is that if we were immortal we shouldn't know that we were alive at all: we know this only because we can contrast our present knowledge that we exist with the fact that we used not to exist, and eventually will no longer exist – but that ontological consideration will be discussed more fully in the final chapter.)

It seems self-evidently the case that the mystery, the inevitability and the finality of death are the prime instigators of belief in God who, by definition, is eternal, and willing, it is hoped, to share eternity with those of his creatures whom he chooses for this reward. There may be a vast range of ideas of what must be done in order to qualify, but the end is the same for all: for those who are accepted, death loses its sting and the grave its victory.

On the face of it, there is a major difference between this circumstance and the others mentioned in this section. While developments in technology and medicine have reduced, if not entirely eliminated, the sense of insecurity and helplessness brought about by disease and other disasters (for example, buildings are now being constructed which are far better equipped to withstand the impact of most earthquakes), death still remains inevitable. By living healthily, and keeping minds and bodies active, we may extend the average life span a little, but it cannot be indefinitely postponed. I suggest, however, that even on this issue there has been a modification in attitude, particularly among the more advanced nations (which must, surely, be followed by the rest eventually). The fact is that, in these nations, while the natural life span may not be getting any longer, *more people are achieving it as time goes by*. Anyone who has attended a funeral will be able to testify that there is much less sorrow over the death of an elderly relative than there is on the occasion of a 'premature' death – of a child from meningitis, an adolescent after a road accident, or a person cut off in his prime by cancer. Where anyone has reached the end of his or her natural life span, the end appears just that – natural. It is the experience of every single species on the planet, and *Homo sapiens* is no exception. We have no reason to doubt that medical research will enable people increasingly to withstand illnesses which prevent them from reaching the natural end of the road. So while the image of death as the grim reaper will never be totally eliminated, the fear of it – meaning the fear of *premature* death, that is, while the faculties are on the whole still in good order – will not be so intense.

A considerable proportion of the fear of death is, in fact, instilled in us by others rather than developed autonomously in our minds. Francis Bacon, in his *Of Death* (1625), expressed this with his usual clarity:

Men fear death as children fear to go in the dark; and as that natural fear in children is increased with tales, so is the other.

Bacon may have been thinking of the so-designated 'men of God' who over the centuries had driven people to turn to God by vividly and terrifyingly describing death and its aftermath. The lust for power by which these acts of persuasion were often motivated is a gigantic scar on Christianity's historical record.

The arguments for the existence of God which have been presented in this chapter fall, in the main, into two distinct categories: those which respond to lacunae, or gaps, in human understanding, and those responding to human incapability. God is introduced as the concept which gives human beings a sense of security in the face of their own fallibility. There remains one further 'proof' which it is difficult to categorise in this way, but has its place in any historical summary of the evidence and is still viewed by many as a key piece of evidence for God's existence and continuing intervention in the world, valid even in our scientific and technological age: *the argument from miracles*:

According to the perspective which brought this argument about, throughout history there have been events or occurrences which are so far different from normal happenings, so apparently supernatural, that they cannot be classified simply as 'rare' or 'inexplicable' or 'exceptional': they are unaccountable, beyond scientific laws, in a word – miraculous. Literally, this word means 'something to wonder at' (from the Latin *mirare*). Thus we have 'the miracle of television', 'the miracle of modern photography', even 'the miracle of the new brassière'. (The batting of Watson and Bailey, who stayed together all day in 1953 to save a test match against the Australians was wittily described the following day in a *Guardian* headline as 'Miracle of faith at Lords'.)

Those who view miracles as indications of divine intervention naturally consider this too weak an interpretation. Miracles are events beyond human ability to comprehend because they are believed to have been caused by a God who is not limited by either human understanding or the laws of nature: he made them both and is therefore perfectly capable of superseding them if he so wills. This he allegedly did when he caused the sun to stand still so that Joshua could finish off more of Israel's enemies, the Amorites (Joshua 10: 13); through Jesus he turned water into wine, multiplied a few loaves and fishes in order to feed a multitude, and raised Lazarus from the dead; and in modern times there has been the miracle of the sole survivor of the Hiroshima bombing; the miracle of Fatima in Portugal in 1917 when the Virgin Mary allegedly appeared to three peasant children, and which still annually attracts pilgrims in their tens of thousands; and of course the numerous reported sightings of the miracle whereby wooden or plastic images of the Virgin weep real tears.

Clearly, if any of these events occurred it would be a miracle. The question is, did they occur? It is an interesting psychological fact that people who are inclined to look for miracles do sometimes conclude that they have experienced one: but that does not establish the truth of their account. We need to take seriously the advice of David Hume apropos of alleged miracles:

> No testimony is sufficient to establish a miracle unless the testimony be of such a kind that its falsehood would be more miraculous than the fact that it endeavours to establish.

On this basis we can reject all the examples cited, with the possible exception of the Hiroshima survival, for which there is the extremely verifiable evidence of the survivor himself. It was certainly a miracle in the sense of something to wonder at, and there the matter rests unless we introduce the concept of God's intervention, in which case we land ourselves in difficulties. If, as about half of the current population of the USA believe, God chose one person in order to reveal that he can do as he wills with his creation (which some people erroneously describe as natural processes), the obvious reaction is to view it as reflecting an odd sense of priorities which allows 50,000 people to die and saves just one: most of us, given the choice, would surely opt for the reverse.

It seems, in fact, to be the case that there are from time to time strange occurrences in the world which are not explicable according to our present knowledge; but this is a totally insufficient reason to introduce God into the equation. It is surely more reasonable to acknowledge that while there is a mystery, we should bear in mind the original meaning of that word and act upon it: *musterion* in Greek means 'that which is waiting to be revealed'.

There are two comments which need to be made about the foregoing 'proofs'. The first has been suggested already: all the arguments presented are examples of a human response to a lacuna in their own knowledge or ability to cope with various life situations. It was this feature which led John Robinson (1963) to criticise them for creating 'a God of the gaps'. He suggested that unless God could be related to areas of human strength rather than where they were weak, few in the future would be willing to believe in him, let alone allow their lives to be guided by him. This line of thought will be followed as the book proceeds, though it will be redirected: for the sake of religion, the belief in God should be dropped not only from areas where we are weak, but also from those in which we are strong.

The second point is more general. A large percentage of both past and present believers in God would have stated quite emphatically – as many still do – that their belief does not rest on anything remotely resembling these arguments; rather, it arises from *experience*: God is real because, quite simply, he reveals himself to them. In the light of that, the arguments for

God's existence, while reassuring in a way, are ultimately superfluous to requirements. And because one person's experience cannot be either analysed or assessed by another person, the only wise response to anyone who states that she *knows* that God exists because she has a personal relationship with him is silence. This claim is, I believe, not false with regard to the actuality of the experience (at least for a proportion of those who make it), but it is a misinterpretation of what occurred. This apparently overwheening statement needs, of course, further elucidation and justification, which will be undertaken in the next chapter.

Chapter 5

Mysticism

That which produces effects within another reality must be termed a reality in itself, so I feel as if we had no philosophic excuse for calling the unseen or mystical world unreal.

(William James, *The Varieties of Religious Experience*)

Our reflections so far enable us to identify what may justifiably be described as three levels of religious experience. First, there is the level of polytheism: the belief that there are many gods active in the world, each having his or her own peculiar responsibilities and areas of authority. We find that, on the whole, this level is appreciated most by unsophisticated people who are encouraged, comforted or challenged by the idea that their welfare comes under the aegis of one particular divine being, whose presence they believe to be symbolised – some might say realised – in a neighbouring shrine, and to whom they can turn when need requires. I shall designate this the lowest level of experience encountered in the world's religions: it is necessary for those of a certain mental status, who need to be able to visualise an idea before it can become a reality in their minds and so have an influence on their lives.

The second level is that of belief in one supreme God, creator, preserver and, for some believers, redeemer of all mankind. This level of belief is, as we have seen, the one expressed by all the theistic religions – Judaism, Christianity, Islam – and over the centuries has probably numbered among its adherents more devotees than would be found at either of the other two levels – a circumstance that could well be still the case. People who express this belief hold that God, the almighty, all-wise and all-loving, is a living reality in their lives. With him they experience a personal relationship which gives shape and purpose to their existence. He is one to turn to in prayer with the assurance that he will hear their concerns, whether their words be of contrition for sins committed, of thanksgiving for mercies received, of petition for others in need, of dedication to his service, of praise for being what he is, or words of dedication, like those of Jesus on the cross: 'Father, into thy hands I commit my spirit' (Luke 23: 46).

The image of God held by these believers is that of a person with whom they can relate at every level of experience. And the experience, as was acknowledged at the end of the previous chapter, is the catalyst of their belief in him. As a headmaster said in a radio debate with me on God's existence: 'I know God exists: he was speaking to me in my car on the way here.' Others affirm that God has entered so deeply into their lives that their values have been transformed, their aims in life radically redirected, cynicism discarded and any mood of despair replaced by optimism, reflecting Leibniz's affirmation that because God is perfect, this is 'the best of all possible worlds'.

It is of course impossible to discuss other people's inner experiences with any degree of confidence. By their very nature, these experiences are integral only to the person concerned, and even he may be confused about what has actually occurred. How can anyone, whether a fellow-believer or an agnostic, make sense of a person's affirmation that God spoke to him that morning? We are at the heart of the problem which underlies all attempts at phenomenological communication between human beings: each representative of the race is in fact, despite the splendid affirmation in Donne's poem, 'an island unto himself alone' and, however strenuously he tries to join the mainland, the best he is ever likely to manage is to be part of an archipelago. The fact is that anyone who describes an alleged personal encounter with God is inevitably building on images of the perfect being which he has been taught, or has read about, prior to the 'encounter'. The emotion that he feels during that experience – and there is often emotion – is therefore characterised as the same kind of personal encounter with a (usually) loving being which has been narrated by countless others. We have already discussed why people *want* to believe that such encounters are possible but it doesn't follow that their description of what occurred – a person-to-Person relationship – is what really happened. If, as I am suggesting, there is no such Person, then any account of a meeting with him must be judged as at best a delusion, at worst an act of deception.

There are two insuperable problems, related but different, with this account of religious experience which make it impossible to characterise it as at the highest religious level. The first, discussed earlier, is the anthropomorphism involved. To say that the God who is encountered possesses certain qualities (normally those reflecting *Homo sapiens* at his best) is to limit God in a way that is inconceivable if he truly is 'that being than which a greater cannot be conceived'. To state that God possesses characteristic X is at the same time to state that he does not possess characteristic not-X, and thus is to limit him, which cannot be the case if he transcends all such distinctions. John Hospers points out (*An Introduction to Philosophical Analysis*, pp. 482–3) that even the use of terms like 'limitless' or 'existing' is putting God in some kind of straightjacket. Thus the God described by those people who claim to have encountered him is not, and never can be, the ultimate ground of being. The answer may well be to the effect that if no epithet can be attached to God, then nothing can be said about him at all. Many religious people have reached that conclusion, as expressed over two millennia ago in the Taoist classic, the *Tao Te Ching*: 'The tao that can be named is not the eternal Tao.' Others side with Boethius in affirming that all we can say about God is *what is he not*.

The second problem arises from the first. The moment a group of people of a particular religion begin to describe God, they inescapably refer to qualities which are uppermost in their own hierarchy of values; a different group will select qualities reflecting their own values, which may differ from those of the first group, as Karen Armstrong's *History of God* highlights.

The 'religious' wars which have plagued the human race over the centuries may not have been fought solely on the issue of whose God is the greatest – race, culture and class have played no small part in bringing these wars about – but the slogan 'dieu et mon droit' has proved a poignant and emotive rallying cry. If the true God is as I – or we – imagine him to be, then anyone whose image of him is different must be judged to be worshipping a lesser being. The very phrase 'my God' (or 'our God', as in 'Our God is marching on') invites antagonism in the name of somebody else's God. (*The Battle Hymn of the Republic* is a call to God to stir himself, as much as the troops. One can almost hear the prayer, 'Cheer up, God, we're coming'.)

So although it is manifestly the case that this second category of religious experience has been well-nigh universal, both geographically and historically, the description of it as an encounter with God, the creator of heaven and earth, is just an example of using imagery which facilitates discussion of the experience. It is precisely because the ultimate cannot be visualised that I view theism as no more than a single step away from polytheism. Both are right in affirming an experience; both are wrong in their explanations of it. 'God' and 'the gods' may have been useful tools for the expression of religious language in the past: but these tools are obsolete and God is dead, however many of his followers still crave to worship the corpse.

The third, and highest, stage in religious experience is one which, by its very nature, is the most difficult to express in words: the mystical. The word mysticism carries the inference of the unknown, the mysterious, even the occult. I shall be suggesting that the mystical experience is available to everybody and, more importantly, has been enjoyed by incalculably more people than actually acknowledge it. First, however, we must examine its nature, as with the other two levels of religious experience, in the context of the world's religions.

It may be defined as a form of direct communion with ultimate reality or spiritual truth, brought about not through the five senses or by any kind of rational process, but by direct intuition, insight or illumination. It involves the loss of personal self-consciousness by a process of what may be termed absorption in the ultimate, the achievement of a non-dualistic state, that is, one in which there is no more 'me' here and 'you', 'that' or 'them' out there: the individual self and the object of the self's consciousness have become one; the state which is reached is then no longer dualistic, but monistic. Thus, to return to the earlier discussion, to say that 'I' encountered 'God' is to remain in a dualistic condition, and this condition remains as long as any spiritual experience is one in which either a personalised God is viewed as the object of devotion, or the devotee is viewed as the object of God's awareness. William James described mysticism as 'a continuum of cosmic consciousness'. In *The Varieties of Religious Experience* (p. 374) he wrote:

> It is that our normal waking consciousness, rational consciousness as we call it, is but one special type of consciousness, whilst all about it, parted only by the filmiest of screens, there lie potential forms of consciousness entirely different. We may go through life without suspecting their existence; but apply the requisite stimulus, and at a touch they are there in all their completeness . . . No account of the universe in its totality can be final which leaves these other forms of consciousness quite disregarded.

With these eidetic words in mind, we shall now look briefly at some of those who have described such an experience in their lives.

The mystics

All the major religions (and most of the minor ones) have produced their mystics. Our present concern remains with those who explored this 'special type of consciousness' within the context of theism (which for many was of course the *only* context available: a highly significant consideration). Not a few of their religious contemporaries, who preferred to follow the well-trodden path of ritual, the sacraments and credal statements, were inclined (and some committed) to the view that the mystics were at best eccentric, at worst heretical. It is easy to imagine the reaction of the ecclesiastical establishment to such words as these spoken in a sermon (of all occasions) by one of the most famous of the mystics, Meister Eckhart (1260–1327):

> When a person has true spiritual experience, he may boldly drop external disciplines, even those to which he is bound by vows.

We have here echoes of the Hindu (and, later, Nietzschean) concept *beyond good and evil*, to be discussed in later chapters. It is worth noting that Meister Eckhart was the inspiration for much of the writing of Søren Kierkegaard, the father of modern existentialism.

The most influential of the early mystics was a teacher whose actual name is unknown, but who wrote under the pseudonym of Dionysius, mentioned in Acts 17: 34 as having been converted to Christianity by St Paul. That it was not he, but instead a person who lived some four or five centuries later, is evinced by the clear expressions of neoplatonism which pervade his teaching.

The neoplatonists, foremost of whom was Plotinus (*c.* 205–270), brought about major modifications in Christian theology, such as a belief in the immortality of the soul rather than the New Testament teaching of the resurrection of the body. Although ascribed to a first-century Christian, Pseudo-Dionysius, then, is normally dated around the sixth century. (To ascribe a work to a famous writer was not usual in the days before printing, when it was often the only way to encourage scribes to engage themselves in the laborious process of making copies: plagiarism in reverse.)

Pseudo-Dionysius, usually known as Denys, takes as his basic stance the fact that God is ineffable, that is, beyond description, beyond words. He would have agreed with the opening of the *Tao Te Ching*, quoted on p. 49: the God that can be talked about is not the ultimate ground of being. God is represented symbolically in the Bible, but only through a series of metaphors, what Denys termed 'poetic imagery'. The words of the Bible, together with the sacraments and the liturgy, are a means whereby the reader or worshipper may be more open to the divine consciousness which pervades all things; the idea that the words spring literally from the mind of God or, even more literally, are the actual words of God dictated to the scribe or prophet was to mistake the channel for the source, just as the contention that the bread and wine used in the eucharist miraculously become the actual body and blood of God as represented in Jesus is to misunderstand the Semitic view of imagery, whereby a symbol both is and, at the same time, is not, that which it symbolises. Denys accepted – at that time and place he could hardly have done otherwise – that the church was always the context for the mystical quest, but he insisted that (as described by John Hick, *The Fifth Dimension*, p. 82) 'the world itself provides further symbols and metaphors of God'.

Included in 'the world' are, of course, human beings; and Denys does not hesitate to use terms which are actually reminiscent of the Jainite philosophy in India, which affirms that our spiritual nature (*jiva*) is the only ultimate reality, so the purpose of each cycle of experience (or incarnation) is to be rid of its opposite, *ajiva*, the body with its material demands. When this is finally achieved we enter into what Jainites term omniscience and, effectively, enjoy eternity in a god-like state. Denys falls short of making such a claim (and, of course, speaks of this life as the only cycle of experience that we shall ever have in this world), but he is not afraid to describe human beings, warts and all, as 'sparks of divinity' seeking to rid themselves of transient material encumbrances in order to enjoy eternal union in the One. Denys remained true to the Christian context of his life by describing the One as God, and by referring to Christian dogma, liturgy and the Bible as supreme aids to the discovery of the mystical path, but we may note at this point that the atheist Shelley spoke of the One in less specific terms:

> The One remains, the many change and pass;
> Heaven's light forever shines, Earth's shadows fly;
> Life, like a dome of many-coloured glass,
> Stains the white radiance of eternity.

> ('Adonais')

It seems not unreasonable to suggest that, had Denys been able to rid himself of the straightjacket in which the theistic ethos and its authorities wrapped him, he would have felt no qualms about those words. He is a pointer on the path to atheistic mysticism.

Some eight centuries later than Denys lived one of the most famous of the Christian mystics, the German Meister Eckhart (1260–c.1328). He was deeply influenced by Denys, but his reflections indicate that he was less dependent than the earlier mystic on the visible manifestations of God as taught by the Church. He made a distinction between God – the perfect being who is the subject of human discourse and debate – and the Godhead: that which, though ultimately responsible for the universe, was essentially indescribable, and could not therefore be the subject of rational debate. Since the Godhead had existed, unknown and undiscussed, for aeons before *Homo sapiens* arrived on the scene, it followed that all discussion of his nature was simply a human conceit whereby basically anthropomorphic ideas were expressed in a more or less self-consistent manner. 'Before there were any creatures,' he said, 'God' (meaning the Godhead) 'was not "God"' (Sermon 52). 'God' came into being only through *Homo sapiens*; before that, all things were united in the Godhead:

> Here is the unity of blades of grass and bits of wood and stone, together with everything else . . . All that nature tries to do is to plunge into that unity, into the Father-nature, so that it may all be one, the Son.

> (Sermon 11)

He boldly takes this concept further in his description of man in relation to God. In his Latin Sermon IV he says:

> If we say that all things are in God, we understand by this that, just as he is without distinction in his nature yet absolutely distinct from all things, so all things are in him in the greatest distinction and yet not distinct, because *man is God in God*. [my italics]

That last statement, unsurprisingly, brought Eckhart into conflict with his superiors, as would no doubt still be the case in many quarters today. It seems that wherever the free spirit which mysticism exemplifies encounters the conservatism expressed in total deferral either to the written word or to the 'truth' as proclaimed by the religious authorities, it risks being treated with extreme caution – or worse. It was G. K. Chesterton, a convert to Roman Catholicism, who described mysticism as 'starting in mist, ending in schism, with an "I" in the middle'. I shall return to this criticism shortly; meanwhile, it is worth recalling that Spinoza, the pantheist, brought excoriation on his head, both from Jews whose company he no longer kept and from Christians whose fellowship he sought but was generally denied, when he wrote of 'God-or-nature' (*deus sive natura*) with the implication that the two are interchangeable. If that concept was deemed an affront to traditional theistic doctrines, how much more so was the concept, with the same implication, 'God-or-man'.

Despite having to exist alongside suspicious colleagues, the mystics continued to be a phenomenon in all the theistic religions. In Christianity it flowered in the West between the eleventh and fourteenth centuries through such memorable figures as St Bernard, St Francis of Assisi, St Bonaventura, St Gertrude, St Thomas Aquinas (none of whom was treated like a saint by most of their contemporaries), Johann Tauler, Meister Eckhart and Jacob Boehme. In England the period produced Richard Rolle, the unknown author of *The Cloud of Unknowing*, Walter Hilton and Dame Julian of Norwich. The golden century of Spanish mysticism was the sixteenth, beginning with Francis of Osuna and Ignatius Loyola, and crowned by St Teresa of Avila and St John of the Cross.

Although Christianity has been particularly rich in its number of mystics, the other theistic religions have not lacked them. Islam has produced the Sufis and Judaism the Cabbalists, even though, like their Christian counterparts, they have been looked upon with suspicion by their more orthodox contemporaries. Evelyn Underhill, in her seminal work *Mysticism* (p. 96) states emphatically that the experience cannot be confined to any one religion:

> Attempts to limit mystical truth – the direct apprehension of the Divine Substance – by the formulae of any one religion, are as futile as the attempt to identify a precious metal with the die which converts it into current coin. The dies which the mystics have used are many . . . But the gold from which this diverse coinage is struck is always the same precious metal: always the same Beatific Vision of a Goodness, Truth, and Beauty which is *one*.

The forms, then, are relative; the substance is absolute.

John Hick (op. cit.) points out that the same distinction between the ultimate, ineffable ground of being and the God of the scriptures and creeds is found both in the Jewish Cabbala and in the writings of the Islamic Al-'Arabi. Jewish Cabbalists distinguished between *Eyn Sof* (the infinite) and the God revealed in scripture. Eyn Sof is unknowable, indescribable: the

God of Abraham, Isaac and Jacob has been comprehensively described. The same is true about Islamic mystics, who distinguish between *al-Haqq* and the revealed God of the Qur'an. Al-'Arabi, for instance, states:

> God is absolute or restricted as He pleases; and the God of religious beliefs is subject to limitations, for He is the God contained in the heart of His servant.
>
> (p. 92)

So mystics from all the three major theistic religions appear to agree that the God whom we can discuss is not the supreme ultimate, who is beyond all discussion. This points the present discussion in a direction which we may tentatively tread here, but with the expectation of being able to march more confidently as we proceed: since we cannot use a name for the ultimate, the word 'God' is superfluous in that context; and since the God we do discuss is not the supreme ultimate, we should cease pretending that he has that status, acknowledge that he is a human creation, and complete the process by dropping the word from our vocabulary. If it is the case that (as Pseudo-Dionysius wrote in *Mystical Theology I*) the mystic 'is enwrapped in that which is altogether intangible and noumenal, being wholly absorbed in Him who is beyond all', then the experience he describes can be – must be – enjoyed in silence, without falling back on anthropomorphisms and analogies.

One feature of mysticism often overlooked is that it has been experienced not only by those whose disposition is towards contemplation, but also by scholars and men of action, with a bent for academic research or public affairs. Pseudo-Dionysius classified mystical experience as either seraphic, cherubic or angelic according to the experience (of God, as the theistic mystics would affirm) as that of one who is to be loved, known, or served. St Teresa, Dame Julian and St John of the Cross are examples of the first group. In her *Revelations of Divine Love*, Dame Julian writes:

> Would you know our Lord's meaning in this thing? Know it well: Love was His meaning. Who showed it you? Love. What did he show you? Love. Why did he show it? For Love.
>
> (p. 86)

Two centuries later, St John of the Cross expresses mystical love even more explicitly:

> A reciprocal love is actually formed between God and the soul, like the marriage union in which the goods of both (the divine essence which each possesses freely by reason of the voluntary surrender between them) are possessed together by both.
>
> (*The Living Flame of Love*, 3: 79)

Other mystics (the cherubic) counted wisdom as the central feature of their experience. Pseudo-Dionysius wrote:

> The All-knowing Mother-Wisdom of the Most High God is superessentially at once the substantiating Cause, the connecting Power, and the universal Consummation of all principles and things.

The same approach is found in the life of Thomas Aquinas, whose *Summa Theologica* remains one of Christianity's great theological expositions. Following in the path of Aristotle, as he did on a whole range of issues, he acknowledged reason as a supreme indication both of God's nature and of his presence in our midst. St Augustine of Hippo, to whom Thomas often defers, wrote in his *Confessions*:

> We did for one instant attain to touch it . . . in a flash of the mind attained to touch the eternal Wisdom which abides over all.
>
> (9, 10 and 23)

The practical (angelic) mystics – people who have balanced their spiritual experiences with a positive commitment to worldly activity – include Mahatma Gandhi and Ignatius Loyola. Ignatius, a soldier before his conversion, was able to harmonise his life by engaging in, on the one hand, regular times of deep contemplation and, on the other, a commitment to aggressive missionary enterprise and proselytising through the Society of Jesus which he founded. His famous prayer asks God to enable us 'To fight and not to heed the wounds; to toil and not to seek for rest; to labour and not to ask for any reward save that of knowing that we do Thy will.' The direction to which that obedience would lead is made explicit in his *Spiritual Exercises*:

> To arrive at the truth in all things, we ought always to be ready to believe that what seems to us white is black if the hierarchical Church so defines it.

Gandhi achieved a balance between action (for him, political action against the British Raj) and withdrawal. He wrote:

> Prayer is not an old woman's idle amusement. Properly understood and applied, it is the most potent instrument of action.
>
> (*Non-Violence in Peace and War*)

As we shall see in the next chapter (p. 63), yoga also accommodates all types of devotees: the scholastic, the contemplative, those engaged in worldly activity or – a significant extension to the celestial hierarchy classified by Pseudo-Dionysius – the artistic. I will make so bold as to categorise this experience of mysticism – remaining within Pseudo-Dionysius's general taxonomy – the archangelic. The word seems not inapposite to describe the mystical experience of artists over the centuries (see Chapter 9).

Criticisms of mysticism

As we have noted here and there, by no means all orthodox theists have felt themselves at ease with mystics and, before moving to study wider manifestations of the phenomenon, we should explore their anxieties. I shall use Chesterton's witty criticism as a guide to these anxieties (see p. 53).

He argues that mysticism 'begins' (and presumably also ends) 'in mist', by which one can deduce that it is suspect because the experience which it describes is vague, indeterminate, and therefore likely to appear wishy-washy to those who prefer precision in their religious expressions. We can accept this as a commendation rather than a criticism. Mysticism is such an intensely personal experience that it is impossible for anyone other than the one involved to be sure of the effect it has.

Aldous Huxley's account of his transformed mental state while under the influence of the drug mescalin, as recounted in *The Doors to Perception*, *seems* to be an account of an experience different from Fritjof Capra's vision of dancing atoms, as related in *The Tao of Physics* (see pp. 101–2), but who can tell with certainty? Who is to know whether the alleged subject of these experiences is deceiving either himself, his audience, or both? The simple fact is that the mystical experience is not open to verification, and therefore is of little value for those seeking from their religion only that which is so open.

It must be doubted whether any mystic would deny the force of these objections, though he would undoubtedly affirm the fact of his experiences even if his interpretation is false: just like a person in love (in fact, with some mystics this analogy is particularly apt). Mysticism may be vague, but are we not surrounded by vagueness, both in our language and in a whole range of experiences? Theists will happily unite in publicly stating their creed, but an analysis of what they actually mean by each credal formula would reveal a wide range of interpretations of the item in the minds of the congregation. What, for instance, do Christians mean when they affirm a belief in Jesus as Son of God? For a son to be born the father's seed must have been shed, but one doubts if that is in the minds of many worshippers. If the phrase is 'symbolic', how many other spiritual leaders (and perhaps not so spiritual) might be entitled to this designation? Most people feel they know what they mean when they make credal affirmations, but on cross-examination would find it virtually impossible to avoid vagueness. It may be argued that this credal item is less vague than are expressions of mysticism because it is possible for the believer to envisage Jesus as he states it: but, again, one wonders whether two people have the same image in their minds.

Vagueness, then, is natural where religious beliefs are concerned; it is also highly desirable since the alternative, precision, creates boundaries and barriers where, by the nature of the subject, none should exist. Precision in religious language is exclusive: it casts non-believers, metaphorically speaking (and, for some, literally), into outer darkness.

It was presumably the need for precision so far as his beliefs were concerned that drove Chesterton into the Roman Catholic Church. There he could no doubt join Ignatius Loyola in calling white black on the command of the ecclesia: certainly, he would have no doubt today about where to stand on the issue of artificial forms of birth control, since the Pope has declared them to be 'intrinsically evil'. Nothing could be less misty than that, surely, yet we have the low birthrate in Italy described on p. 42. If His Holiness had been wise enough to shroud his views on sexual behaviour in a haze, how many more might have given him a hearing. Many others look for precision through the written word, arguing that, amid all these troubled and changing times, the Word of God remains unambiguous, uncompromised, unassailed. So we know where we stand on homosexuality, since Leviticus 18: 22 states conclusively: 'You shall not lie with a male as with a woman; it is an abomination.' We can put the feminists in their place with the equally unmisty instruction of St Paul: 'I permit no woman to teach or to have authority over men; she is to keep silent' (1 Timothy 2: 12). And if we're worried about marital infidelity, we can turn to the Qur'an: 'The adulterer and the adulteress, scourge ye each of them with 100 stripes. And let not pity for the twain withhold you from obedience to Allah.' Precision is confined to the mores of a particular time and place: to expect it when we are concerned with the timeless and universal is to express a naivety which only ignorance or insecurity can create.

Chesterton's identification of the 'I' in the middle is a fair comment, and would have been more apt if it could be shown that mystics generally have been indifferent to the needs of those around them, as can be disproved simply by reading their life stories. That the experience is intensely personal no one will deny, but one is entitled to wonder when this was seen as deleterious to religion. Eckhart's statement that the experience takes its recipient beyond good and evil and above vows *sounds* egotistic, but only to one who hasn't taken the trouble to explore what is really meant by that apparent braggartry. It is significant that Kierkegaard felt drawn to these sentiments during his own religious quest, and declared that for him faith was a personal leap in the dark, unaided by creeds or theological niceties. (He, too, was viewed with suspicion by his fellow churchmen.) The suggestion that many religious people are not sure enough in their faith to make such a leap, and that they need the crutches of biblical verses and ecclesiastical statements in order to gain a modicum of security in their beliefs is acceptable: they are entitled to state that mysticism is beyond them, but this does not entitle them to mouth the glib criticisms of the mystical experiences which they hear expressed by many who have not reached that state in their spiritual journeys. Some words from the *Tao Te Ching* (which we shall examine in Chapter 8) are apposite:

> When a superior man hears of the Tao,
> he immediately begins to embody it.
> When an average man hears of the Tao,
> he half believes it, half doubts it.
> When a foolish man hears of the Tao,
> he laughs out loud.
> If he didn't laugh,
> it wouldn't be the Tao.

(p. 41, Stephen Mitchell translation)

Chesterton's reference to schism apropos of mysticism was added no doubt to complete his *bon mot*. Far from being schismatic (except in the minds of those at a different spiritual level who wish to separate themselves from the mystics), mysticism is a unifying element in religion, found, as we have seen, among theistic religions but experienced, as we shall see, in both the non-theistic religions and orbits beyond those of formal religious activities and beliefs. It may be contended that, being beyond rational explanation, it is beyond reasoned discussion, and should therefore be included in Wittgenstein's topics 'whereof (we must) be silent'. Our aim, however, is not to reveal how it works – an impossible task – but to indicate the contexts in which it has been experienced so as to broaden out the company of those who may be described as religious.

Chapter 6

Non-dualism in Hinduism

> As therefore the individual soul and the highest Self differ in name
> only . . . it is senseless to insist (as some do) on a plurality of Selfs, and to
> maintain that the individual soul is different from the highest Self.
>
> (Adi Shankara, *Commentary on the Vedanta Sutras*, 1, 22)

Hinduism is the most comprehensive of the world's religions. It embraces
every level of belief outlined in Chapter 3, from polytheism through theism
to mysticism (or non-theism). There are two reasons why this is not surprising. The first is the geographical factor: 'Hindu', is the Hindi word for India,
so the designation 'Hinduism' embraces the religious beliefs of an entire
subcontinent. The second is the historical factor: the most ancient writings of
Hinduism (and therefore held to be the most authoritative), the Vedas, date
from at least as early as 1500 BCE, and some scholars place the earliest writings up to half a millennium earlier still. When we add to these the writings
of the so-called Epic Period (*c.* 500 BCE–*c.* 150 CE), such as the Upanishads
(which are actually the latest of the Vedas but are usually considered independently), the *Mahabharata* (with its crowning glory the *Bhagavad-gita*),
the *Ramayana* and the Yoga Sutras of Patanjali, it is not surprising that a
vast range of differing religious concepts are expressed. So we find expressions of devotion to Brahman, Vishnu, Shiva and his consort Kali, Krishna
and many more gods and demigods.

On the other hand, the belief is expressed that, while Vishnu and Shiva
(for example) have certain specific responsibilities (Vishnu the preserver of
the world, Shiva its destroyer, including the destroyer of evil), Brahman, the
creator, is the ultimate divine authority. Here, there is a parallel with the distinction made by Meister Eckhart between God, or gods, who is/are
manifestations of divinity in the world – in nature, or the scriptures, or religious communities, for example – and the Godhead who or which is
unknowable, so that, in Hick's words (op. cit., p. 89) it 'opens the door to
the distinction between the Real and its plurality of manifestations'. Eckhart

did not go through this door but many Hindu scholars and teachers, unfettered by ecclesiastical authorities or their equivalent, have boldly followed the paths to which it led.

One of these paths led them to a viewpoint not far removed from the theistic beliefs of Judaism, Christianity and Islam. Their view that secondary gods represent the supreme God, Brahman, in various forms gives Hindu expressions of theism a distinctive emphasis, but no Western theist would object to these words from the *Bhagavad-gita* (11, 38):

Thou art the Primal God, the Ancient Spirit,
Thou art the Supreme Treasure-house of this universe,
Thou art the knower, and the known, the highest Home,
By thee the universe is pervaded, O thou of infinite form.

The significant feature of this profession of belief, so far as our present study is concerned, is that the relationship between Brahman and the worshipper is dualistic, like that between God and his Jewish, Christian and Muslim worshippers. That is to say, there remains a two-way process between God on the one hand, and his people on the other. He instructs them, they pray to him. Some of the mystics of the theistic religions come very near to passing beyond this dualism, but always hold back from taking the final step. They speak of absorption in God, but it is an absorption which does not obliterate their individual selves. They were bold enough to offer the image of the individual as a drop of water, to be absorbed into the wine of God. The drop would certainly be absorbed in the wine (which is, in any case, mainly water): but it needs no chemist (or drinker) to confirm that water is not wine. So, following the analogy through, however deeply any human being may believe herself to be pervaded by the spirit of God, she remains a human being: saintly, perhaps; transformed, perhaps; but a human being none the less; the condition *vis-à-vis* God remains dualistic. Suppose, however, the image were changed to one in which a drop of water were absorbed in a glass of *water*: the implications of that image are so far-reaching that they take us beyond any boundaries so far explored, even the widely extended boundaries of the theistic mystics. It invites us to see ourselves not just as sharing in God's nature, but in his being; to recognise that the ground and source of the universe can be found in each individual, so that everyone can confidently affirm, 'Tat tvam asi'. This is usually translated as 'thou art that'; but, as mentioned on p. 16, there are other interpretations of this mystical expression: 'I am that'; 'all this is that'; 'there is nothing but that'. We thus enter a different form of thought from any considered so far, taking us to the heart of Hinduism.

Advaita Vedanta

There are six orthodox 'systems' (*upangas*, literally 'high limbs') in Hinduism, all gaining their orthodoxy through their devotion to the Vedas. *Nyaya*, literally 'going into a subject', is concerned mainly with logic and epistemology; *Vaisesika*, literally 'referring to the distinctions', is more scientific than philosophical, indicating how the many facets of nature may be divided into six categories; *Sankya*, literally 'pertaining to number', teaches that the universe consists of a union between *prakriti* (nature) and *purusha* (consciousness or, loosely, spirit); *Yoga*, literally 'yoking', shows how this union may be effected in any human being; *Mimamsa*, meaning 'investigation', embraces two systems: *Purva-*, or 'older-' Mimamsa is mainly concerned with ritual, while *Uttera-* or 'later-' Mimamsa relates to knowledge of the truth. This last system is generally known as *Vedanta*, hence the earlier system is now generally simply called Mimamsa. While Vedanta will be our primary concern, it should be noted that its teaching pervades all the systems, which are viewed by Hindus as facets of the diamond of truth, not as rivals in its expression.

Through the writings of Western authors such as Aldous Huxley and Christopher Isherwood, and Indian gurus and scholars like Ramakrishna (1834–86), Vivekananda (1863–1902) and, more recently, Sarvepalli Radhakrishnan (1888–1975), Vedanta has made a considerable impact on the West over the last century. Radhakrishnan wrote of it in *Indian Philosophy* (1962):

> Of all the Hindu systems of thought, the Vedantic philosophy is the most closely connected to Indian religion and in one or another form it influences the world view of every Hindu thinker of the present time.

Vedanta means 'crown' (or end) of the Vedas. It is normally preceded by the defining adjective 'advaita', meaning 'non-dualistic' ('dvaita' means dualistic with the prefix indicating the opposite). The great exponent of this system was Adi Shankara (788–820), particularly in his commentary on the *Vedanta-sutra* (sutra means 'thread' or (relatively) brief writings) *Shariraka-Bhashya*. He was a saint, a scholar, a poet, a philosopher, a reformer and, central to our exploration, a mystic.

Shankara suggested that in order to understand what advaita means we should take a hard look at human experience. He taught – what all people must know to be true – that there are three daily recurring states of consciousness. First, there is *dreaming sleep*, characterised by partial awareness and duality: the duality indicated by the fact that in dreams the subject-object condition remains, the dreamer aware of him- or herself reflecting on the dream. Second, there is the *awakened state*, characterised by duality and ordinary awareness. This is the duality of the perceiver and the perceived, and one's awareness of this as a recurring experience. Third, we all experience *deep or dreamless sleep*: this is characterised by the unity of non-dualism and unawareness. These three states are symbolised in Hindu writings as A, U and M, making the sound OM. But according to Shankara's interpretation of advaita there is a fourth state, called simply *turiya* or *the fourth*, which is characterised by both awareness and non-dualism, a state in which there is no longer both perceiver and perceived, a subject of consciousness and its object, but the unity, the oneness, of absorption. In the West, and throughout this book, we have termed this state mystical; Hindus call it *samadhi*, literally meaning 'to establish or make firm', signifying the total absorption of the subject in the object of meditation.

There are a number of stages of samadhi, the highest being *nirvikalpasamadhi*, 'changeless samadhi', which refers to the highest transcendent state of consciousness. Assuming that Brahman is the object of meditation, it is the state of enlightenment which happens when a person can say, beyond any doubt, 'I am Brahman'. This concept may have occupied the meditator's conscious mind over many years; it may have been a matter of debate and speculation; but at the moment of enlightenment it becomes a matter of certitude. Having experienced the condition in which there is no longer mind, duality, or the subject-object relationship, he *knows*: and nothing can ever thereafter remove or lessen this assurance. Shankara illustrates with a vivid picture the fact that, once gained, enlightenment can never be lost. He describes a man sitting in a cell-like darkened room. It is too dark to see anything clearly, but he dimly perceives, at the far end of the room, a deadly snake hanging from the window. He sits motionless in terror, knowing that if the snake becomes aware of his presence it may make for him, bite him and cause him to die in appalling agony. Then, just for a moment, there is a shaft of light, and in that moment he recognises the 'snake' for what it really is: nothing more than a piece of rope, a window-sash. The light disappears and the near-darkness returns. But now he is at peace with his situation, knowing that he has nothing to fear. He can gaze at the window, now dimmed, and tell himself how understandable it had been to mistake the rope for a snake. Friends may call to warn him that he is in deadly danger, but he can laugh at their fears. Having experienced the moment of enlightenment (in Sanskrit, *moksha*) nothing and nobody can shatter his tranquillity, since he knows the truth of the situation.

Shankara doesn't explain how the moment of enlightenment occurs, why it happens to some and not to others, and why now rather than then. The confidence that seeps through his writings, reflecting the assurance of the whole Vedanta school, is that ultimately all will attain this state. Of course, Hinduism teaches the doctrine of reincarnation, implying that we have potentially an indefinite number of cycles of experience before us. Meanwhile, by reflection and meditation, we may so dispose ourselves that we are ready to enter 'the fourth' at any time.

For some this state will become more real than the awakened state. In his
Philosophies of India (p. 376), Heinrich Zimmer writes:

> Through his [the yogin's] sovereign yogic power the gross aspect of real-
> ity (that is, the ordinary state of awakenness) is, for him, devaluated; for
> he can produce the subtle, fluid forms of the inward state of vision
> whenever he likes, fix them and retain them as long as he requires, and
> after that, again according to his wish, come temporarily back into
> touch with the exterior world. Such a virtuoso is not subject and
> exposed helplessly to the waking state, but enters into it only when and
> as he wishes – his real abode or homestead, meanwhile, being the
> 'fourth' at the opposite end of the series.

The frequency with which a person enters this state, and the length of time
spent in it, are both ultimately irrelevant. As we saw with the categorisation
of theistic mystics, there will always be some whose lives are centred more on
academic or practical, social, even political pursuits than on contemplation.
Yoga takes account of this, with its variety of types: jnana yoga is the yoga
of knowledge; karma yoga of action; bhakti yoga, devotion: all are contained
within the quest for samadhi, and no one need feel that the only way to
enlightenment is that of contemplation. The parallel with Denys' three categories is clear.

Atman and Brahman

At the heart of the non-dualistic experience, Shankara argued, are the Atman
and Brahman. Brahman (not to be confused with brahmin, which is the
name for the priestly caste in the Hindu social system) is difficult to express
in Western terms without begging a number of questions. 'Ultimate reality'
is one term that has been used, and 'holy power' another. The Vedanta uses
the formula *sat-chit-ananda*, meaning being-consciousness-bliss, which is
not a very felicitous phrase. Perhaps the best translation, if only because it is
the most straightforward and comprehensible, is *ground of being*.

What this phrase implies is that Brahman is the underlying source of
everything that either is or exists (assuming that we can distinguish between
these two concepts, discussed on p. 38); this is implied in the 'being-con-
sciousness' part of the tripartite formula. Brahman has being – is – eternally;
without Brahman's creative energy there would be no universe: the black
hole would have remained permanently in that state. Brahman will therefore
endure when all that we encounter has ceased to be and when God and the
gods have disappeared from the scene. As the Upanishads (1,4,6) state:

> This that people say: 'Worship this god' 'Worship that God!' one after
> another – this is (Brahman's) creation indeed! And he himself is all the gods.

So far this thinking has not taken us much further than the distinction between God and the Godhead made by Meister Eckhart. It is in the teaching about Atman and its relationship with Brahman that Advaita Vedanta opens up a discourse at a new level of experience. Atman can be translated as 'soul', but this would be inadequate since it can mean 'body', 'mind' or 'soul' according to the circumstances. Ninian Smart, in his *The Religious Experience of Mankind*, describes it as the 'still centre' from which an individual's thoughts, feelings and actions proceed. It is a person's individual entity, his or her basic being, from which their 'field of being' (Heidegger's phrase) extends. In the teaching of Advaita, it is identified in sound by the three letters which, as we have seen, symbolise the three states of every human being: A,U,M, creating the sound OM. Thus the Atman combines the states of dreaming sleep, dreamless sleep, and the awakened state in one self (and the word 'self' could stand as the most succinct translation of Atman). But there is more than this, since the fourth state, the state of enlightenment, is lacking. Because this is a state of silence, no sound needs to be added: OM can represent either just the first three or all four states of consciousness coexisting in one person, and together they describe Atman. The Mandukya Upanishad draws these concepts together and leads us forward to the climax of this thinking in these words:

> What is known as the fourth portion – neither inward- nor outward-turned consciousness, nor the two together; not an undifferentiated mass of dormant omniscience; neither knowing nor unknowing – because invisible, ineffable, intangible, devoid of characteristics, inconceivable, undefinable, its sole essence being the assurance of its own Self; the coming to peaceful rest of all differentiated, relative existence; quiet, peaceful-blissful; without-a-second (advaitam, non-dualistic): this is Atman, the Self, which is to be realised.

Anyone reading these descriptions of Atman and Brahman may justifiably ask what the difference is between the two concepts. The answer is, basically none at all. To return to, but to change radically, an image mentioned earlier, the Atman may be described as a drop of water and Brahman as the ocean, and any person's entry into the fourth state means that he or she has realised the portentous truth of this. The *Bhagavad-gita* states:

> He who knows himself in everything and everything in himself will not injure himself by himself.

Shankara used a similar image: just as there is no essential difference between the air inside a jar and the air outside (they are separated from each other only by the artificiality of the jar), so there is no essential difference between the individual Atman and the universal Brahman. This is the claim made in the central text of the Upanishads, already quoted: *Thou art that*: it is the claim that Atman and Brahman are one; that any person's individual being permeates the Ground of being, which pervades and actuates the whole universe. As salt dissolved in water flavours all the water (to use yet another image) so does Atman pervade Brahman; and this is the 'bliss', the third of the essential features of Brahman presented in the formula *sat-chit-ananda*. The Upanishads (6,9,4) state this concept simply and pithily:

> That which is the finest essence – this whole world has that as its soul. That is Reality. That is Atman. *That art thou.*

The belief expressed in Advaita Vedanta is that all will finally attain this state of enlightenment. Without having a belief in reincarnation, this seems optimistic; but any Hindu would say that this highest of all states is worth pursuing more than anything else during this present cycle of experience even – or especially – if it is the only one we shall know. If at the end we are to be one with Brahman, the ground of being, the soul of the universe, then a foretaste could well be worth seeking, in the confidence (or hope) that the silence of the fourth state will make the other three states redundant (so that the sound OM is no longer heard). We may return to the passage already quoted (p. 64) from the Mandukya Upanishad and add its dynamic conclusion (possibly the most famous verse in the Vedas):

> Thus OM is Atman, verily. He who knows thus merges his Self in the Self – yea, he who knows thus.

This is no submerging of the person in the infinity of the Godhead, as described in the writings of the theistic mystics; it is not a water drop absorbed into the wine. At the peak of Hindu mysticism, with the realisation of the Atman, is the assurance that all that can be said about Brahman can be said about the individual self: what the Brahman is, *that am I*.

This statement will be heresy in the minds of biblical and ecclesiastical fundamentalists, but, in fact, it is the only realistic way – and, more important, the only natural way – to realise the divine: not as something 'out there' to be held in awe, but as the catalyst of the drive which is to be found in any individual if he or she so wishes (or, perhaps, as his or her eyes have so been opened). 'He who has seen me has seen the Father', said Jesus (John 14: 9): he speaks for all who have gained enlightenment, and if Christianity could realise that truth instead of, on the one hand, falling back on an assinine literalism which reduces *Homo sapiens* to a condition of cringing subservience or, on the other, losing its sense of direction by trying to be so many things to so many people that it becomes very little to very few, it could join with those who boldly confess their own divinity, knowing that though they will surely die, they will never *know death*. The words which St Anselm used about God can (in fact) be applied to each separate person: 'There never was a time when *I* was not, and there never will be a time when *I* will not be.' Why this is ontologically realistic and not as crazy as it sounds will be discussed in the final chapter. Meanwhile, we can acknowledge that Hinduism, at its highest, introduces human beings to a religion where God is redundant, and men and women take his place. Not all Hindus make that affirmation; many hold back and retain the concept of dvaita – dualism – in place of advaita. But it is difficult to avoid the conclusion that the future of religion, whether in Hinduism, or in any other 'religion', lies with non-dualism. We shall see in Chapter 9 that this is an experience shared by many who are outside the confines of any of the world's religions.

Chapter 7

Buddhism

> If you realise perfect wisdom for a single moment, then the whole truth is known to you. And perfect wisdom can only be realised for a single moment.
>
> (Hui-neng, Zen Master, *c.* 700)

Buddha means 'enlightened person', and Buddhists follow the teaching of one who was particularly enlightened, Siddhartha Gautama (564–484 BCE). He was born into a noble family of the Shakya clan in what is now Nepal, married and had a son, then, at the age of twenty-nine, left home and entered the state of homelessness, which meant abandoning all family and social ties. Seeking spiritual liberation, he first turned to ascetic teachers but, finding asceticism to be spiritually unrewarding, turned to meditation. At the age of thirty-five he spent forty-nine days under a tree (now known as the Bodhi tree) in the village of Gaya (now Bodh-Gaya) and realised complete enlightenment. At first he remained silent about his experience, since he felt it impossible to communicate it to others, but eventually, at the request of would-be followers, he began to teach. He spent the remainder of his life travelling from place to place, and gathered a large number of disciples, who called him Shakyamuni, or '(silent) sage of the Shakya clan'. After his death he was usually called, simply and uniquely, Buddha, though he had seen himself as just one of countless enlightened persons who appear in every age and society. In the centuries after his death his message spread throughout the whole of south-east Asia – through Burma, Vietnam, Cambodia, Laos, Thailand and Sri Lanka. Eventually, it spread further afield, to China, Japan, Tibet, Mongolia and, later, to the West, where, in one form or another, it is a thriving religion (there are today more Buddhist communities in Bristol, England, one of John Wesley's main centres, than there are Methodist).

Those are the bare historical bones of Buddhism, which ironically is followed outside India rather than in the subcontinent in which it originated. (In fact, the relationship between it and Hinduism is in some ways similar to that between Christianity and Judaism.) To orthodox Hindus it is viewed to be *nastika* – heterodox. There are numerous reasons for this judgment, but the main one is Buddha's claim to have received enlightenment without recourse to their most authoritative scriptures, the Vedas; and that his enlightenment gave him the authority to branch off on his own path. So he was held to be unorthodox, but the Hindus showed their respect for him by naming him as one of the incarnations of their god, Vishnu, the preserver, whom they believed to reappear in any age where material values were swamping the spiritual. Unorthodoxy did not mean heresy.

Buddhism's diaspora, or dispersion, causes a major problem for anyone trying to give an account of its teaching. In south-east Asia it remained reasonably faithful to its origins, and it is mainly there that the Theravada school of Buddhism – the only surviving school of the group originally designated 'Hinayana', or 'lesser (narrow) vehicle' – is found. This school has tried to maintain intact the original teaching of Buddha. As Buddhism travelled further afield, however, it encountered indigenous religious traditions as old as, or older than, its own. In the process of establishing itself, it is not to be wondered at that there was some modification of the original teaching, some element of syncretisation, which led to the development of a variety of forms of Buddhism – Pure Land Buddhism in China, for example, Zen Buddhism in Japan and, above all, in Tibet, where the autochthonous religions of both nature worship and *bon* (relating to divination and rites for the dead) were widely followed. In these countries – and today, for the most part, in the West – a different Buddhism expressed itself from that found in the Theravada tradition: Mahayana, or 'greater vehicle', in which the original teaching of Buddha (contained in what today is called the Dharmapada) was extended (some might say watered down) so as to include both the richest insights of the indigenous religions and the ideas of Buddhist scholars, such as Nagarjuna in the second or third century, who expanded Buddha's teaching along paths which he had not followed. The result, with the notable exception of Zen Buddhism, was a return to many of the theistic and polytheistic beliefs of earlier societies, and therefore has no contribution to make to our own exploration. It is only in the Theravada tradition, together with its scion, Zen, that we can be most confident of finding what Buddha originally proclaimed. And this was so revolutionary that many latter-day followers have still to take it into their systems; for what Buddha had to say was that there is no God and that human beings have no souls.

Theravada Buddhism

'No soul' is the literal translation of one of the three marks of existence which Buddha identified. The first was *duhkha*, or suffering, including (or especially) mental pain born of frustration, anxiety, despair and unfulfilment;

the second was *anicca* or *anitya*, impermanence, which is the condition of everything and every creature which exists. Buddha's last words were, 'Decay is inherent in all creatures. Strive diligently', which indicates how central to Buddhist thought is this feature. The third mark is *anatta* or, in Sanskrit, *anatman*. We discussed in the previous chapter the meaning of 'Atman', the self, and the Vedanta claim that it is essentially the same as Brahman, the ground of being. In Buddhism we have the opposite concept: anatman means no Atman, hence no self, no soul. Mahayana reached back to the original Hinduism and retained a belief in the soul; but it is alien to original Buddhist teaching. The word 'anatman' is unambiguous. According to Buddha, nothing endures, not even the individual self; we are, in the words of a book of that title by Stephen Collins, *selfless persons*.

This teaching has important implications for the interpretation of the state to which, Buddha taught, all experience and all incarnations led: nirvana. Later Buddhists spoke of this along the lines of paradise in Islamic and Christian thought, but that, again, is to depart from the word's actual meaning, which is 'blowing out', as of a candle flame. Just as one cannot describe where the flame has gone after being blown out, except that it has entered a different dimension from that of its previous existence, so no more can be said about the condition of nirvana than about its location. Buddha himself was reticent when asked about it, telling his disciples that they would know when they entered it: but it is difficult to avoid the conclusion, especially when suffering and decay are viewed as the other two inescapable marks of existence, that nirvana means non-existence or annihilation. Here, for illustration, is a description of Buddha's death in a sutra written shortly afterwards, the Maha Parinibbana Sutra (6, 8–9):

> The Buddha went into the first stage of meditation, and then quickly into the second and third stages. Finally, he went into the fourth stage of meditation, after which he entered the sphere of the infinity of space.
>
> He passed out of the sphere of the infinity of space, and entered the sphere of the infinity of consciousness. And passing out of the sphere of the infinity of consciousness, he entered the sphere of nothingness. And passing out of the sphere of nothingness, he entered the sphere in which there is neither perception nor non-perception. And passing out of the sphere in which there is neither perception nor non-perception, he entered into the sphere where all experience of perception ceases . . . Shortly afterwards, Buddha passed from the sphere where all experience of perception ceases, and entered nirvana.

It is difficult not to feel that the final phrase in that description could be replaced with our more familiar 'and passed away'. To what, we cannot tell, but if we are to take Buddha at his word, it was not to a state of continuing awareness. As he said, outlining only what nirvana was *not*, 'In this condition there is no self; and that which is without self is hard to understand.' Buddha is consequently viewed by the Theravada school as having been removed from our dimension so as to be available to us only (though it is a major 'only') through his inspirational teaching and example.

The concepts of nirvana and anatman, then, remain shrouded in vagueness and are therefore indescribable. More unequivocal is the lack of reference to Brahman in Buddha's teaching. The quest for nirvana, which, as we shall see, is furthered primarily by non-attachment and meditation, is a pursuit for each individual, and Brahman does not enter into the equation. Here, of course, Buddha departed from the Hinduism which was his earliest belief – even the non-dualism of Vedanta – and, like his Jainite contemporaries, argued that the spiritual path was one which depended on constancy of purpose in the minds of each follower, whom he advised to 'work out (their) own salvation'. He assured them that there was no God to aid them in their quest, avowing that even if there were any gods, anybody who realised nirvana was in a higher state than they. There is, in fact, a strong existentialist thread in Buddha's teaching, which called for autonomy, authenticity, personal responsibility and the avoidance of what Sartre called 'bad faith', which for Buddha meant hiding behind the mask of conventional religion.

Why, then, is Buddhism included among the world's religions? Without a God or a soul (except in its wider, syncretistic manifestations), should it not rather be regarded as a psychological method for coping with the frustrations and miseries of life? There seems no reason to deny this. In his advice to his followers to stop hankering after what the world can provide, and to instead build up an inner being which is independent of outer rewards, to cease the fruitless grasping after that which cannot ultimately satisfy because it cannot endure, he was giving counsel which has since put countless minds at ease. One commentator remarked somewhat sardonically that the main contribution of Buddhism was to enable people to live with sod's law: if things can go wrong, they will. It may be this element in his teaching which has created so wide a response in the West, whose only indigenous philosophy is a stark and ultimately destructive materialism. Buddhism, in fact, offers a common-sense approach to material possessions and human relationships (which are just as transient as physical delights): not to become ascetics, the way of the Jains, which Buddha rejected, but to follow what is now known as the Middle Way, the way of detachment. It means reaching a state where envy of others has been obliterated and people are content with their lot (even while seeking to improve it). The path to happiness means, among other things, being unable to answer the question, often put in questionnaires, 'What single addition in your life would make you happy?', because this question, tautological though this may seem, is question-begging.

However, Buddha charged his monks to spend a large proportion of their time in meditation, and it is by this process that the genuinely religious aspect of Buddhism is manifested. He suggested that anyone – layperson as

well as monk – would be taking the surest steps towards nirvana if they followed his directions in what has for long been known as the Noble Eightfold
Path. Having found a quiet place, whether indoors or out, they should sit
comfortably and concentrate, which means banishing from the mind any
hindrances to deeper meditation. What this implies is outlined in one of the
sutras of the *Pali Canon* (which are the only writings held to be authoritative
by Theravada Buddhists), the Samanna-phala Sutra (67–8):

> He sets aside all hankering for the world. He purifies himself of all
> desires. He suppresses any urge to injure other living beings. He frees his
> mind from all anger and malice. He lifts his heart and mind from torpor.
> He sharpens his perceptions. He banishes indolence and sloth, anxiety
> and worry, irritability and vexation. He transcends confusion, perplex-
> ity and doubt.

In other words, in order to meditate one must be calm, forget about external duties, not be in a state of doziness or anxious about trivial matters and,
above all, be confident that this activity is valuable both for its own sake and
for that to which it may lead. Having overcome these hindrances, the mind
becomes increasingly tranquil and self-possessed, leading to a state beyond
any considerations of well-being and suffering, where there is, in the words
of the sutra, 'purity of awareness, perfect equanimity, and utter self-posses-
sion'. In transcendent moments like these, the meditator will know how
valid are the Four Noble Truths, and realise beyond doubt that suffering can
be overcome by the cessation of craving. The layperson will return to worldly
concerns, of course, but these moments of tranquillity and illumination will
enable him or her to evaluate them differently: he or she will have found that,
by harmonising activity with passivity, priorities in life are more felicitously
established. Beyond this, it may be possible to enter into a deeper level of
awareness and appreciate more fully that our experience of time is, in fact,
eternal, as suggested on p. 65. Once that is known, the question of what, if
anything, survives after the death of the body becomes of no consequence.
Through the deeper experiences of meditation, each practitioner can find
that he or she is experiencing eternity now, and this knowledge can trans-
form the rest of their activities. This may not be religion as biblical and
ecclesiastical theists describe it, but one cannot contemplate describing this
as anything other than a religious experience: and it is religion without God.
Buddha said:

> *By my own spiritual exertions* [my italics] I learn that enlightenment is
> beyond the sphere of nothingness; . . . It is the sphere where there is ces-
> sation of perception, and hence cessation of all attachment.

The thought patterns which underlie this account may not suit all, but many throughout the world are finding in Buddhism a way of coping with anxiety and stress which is more realistic than the theistic religions' assurances about divine love and empathy. Here the world is recognised for what it is, unredeemed and unredeemable. With this view, theistic myths are superfluous to requirements.

Zen Buddhism

What Theravada Buddhism forged, Zen Buddhism honed and fine-tuned. It began through the ministry in China (where it is named by its Chinese transliteration, Ch'an) of Bodhidharma around the sixth or seventh century. He was the twenty-eighth Indian patriarch after Shakyamuni Buddha and, so tradition has it, began his ministry in China by spending nine years facing a wall in deep meditation, known as *zazen*. After this long period, many enquirers came to him, and Buddhism became established in China alongside two native traditions, Taoism and Confucianism.

Zen is the Japanese version of the Sanskrit word *dhyana*, the highest point of the Noble Eightfold Path.[1] It refers to the collectedness of mind or meditative absorption which occurs when all dualistic distinctions, such as those between I and thou, subject and object, true and false, are eliminated. In this there are clear parallels with Advaita Vedanta. Unlike the Hindu non-dualistic system, however, Zen speaks not of a state of unity between the self and Brahman (neither of which Buddhism believes to exist), but of a process of awareness leading to complete awakening as experienced by Buddha under the Bodhi-tree. This experience is available to all, so that untold numbers since the time of Shakyamuni Buddha have taken his title. Zen is, in fact, often termed the 'School of Buddha Mind'.

The word used in Zen for enlightenment is *satori*, from the root 'to know'. This is not knowledge gained empirically, but intuitive knowledge, arrived at by no identifiable or logical procedures. Because there are no 'well-worn steps' to satori, it is impossible to say how long a practitioner, monk or layperson, will have to spend in zazen before achieving it. Zen novices (a status that can last for many years) will be guided by a Zen Master, but when the moment comes, it will be like a bolt from the blue (not unlike Shankara's man with the rope). More than any other school of thought or religion which we shall examine, Zen teaches that meditation, zazen, is the only sure way to enlightenment. Everything else, however strongly associated with one religion or another, is viewed as little more than lumber, more a hindrance than a help along the way.

Much play is made in Zen on the intuitive nature of satori. It is often likened to an archer's hitting the target without taking aim, suggesting that anybody in that, or any other sport, who starts *thinking* about what he is doing, instead of performing spontaneously and unthinkingly, will not achieve his best standard. Players of musical instruments will confirm this experience from their own sphere of activity: the best playing happens when the performer is so absorbed in the music that he no longer considers the *how* but only the *what*. It is this self-consciousness which Zen views as the major component of the lumber, and much of Zen teaching is about ways to overcome it.

There are three practices in particular, all of them central features in most of the world's religions, which Zen warns against if satori is to be achieved. The first of these is *dependence on ritual*. Hinduism had declared dharma to be a hindrance in the pursuit of moksha, along with *artha* (wealth) and *kama* (pleasure); and dharma embraces both formal teaching and public worship. Hindu teachers were concerned about how easily a person could persuade himself that because he was a regular attender at a particular place of worship, his spiritual condition must be sound. Hindus warn that, while this may be the case (attendance at the liturgy may accompany regular periods of private meditation) *it also may not*, because it is clearly possible for a person to go through the motions of the liturgy without feeling in the slightest way involved in the event. (I recall singing one of Wesley's most devout hymns alongside a very famous colleague who turned to me between the lines 'Hide me, O my Saviour, hide,' and 'O receive my soul at last' with the words 'What do you think of that damn fool so-and-so? Still thinks he's a hell of a fellow'.)

Zen Buddhists go further than this Hindu cautionary approach, however, and declare ritual to be a definite barrier to the pursuit of satori. Even to recite the words of an earlier master was viewed by Mumon Ekai, a twelfth-century master, as a sign of having left the path; and Hui-neng, the seventh-century Zen patriarch, stated, 'Those who think that perfect wisdom can be realised by studying external objects, will never realise perfect wisdom.'

The second example of lumber to be discarded as a refuge for the pusillanimous was any kind of *dependence on sacred texts*. Again this view had been foreshadowed in Hinduism: the *Bhagavad-gita* states (II, 46):

> As much profit as there is in a water-tank
> when on all sides there is a flood of water,
> No more is there in all the Vedas
> For a Brahman who (truly) understands.

Bold words indeed within a context which defined unorthodoxy as primarily an unwillingness to accept the authority of the Vedas. The same idea is expressed in Zen, again by Mumon (28):

> The teachings of the sacred texts are very profound. But compared with enlightenment, they are like a single hair in comparison with the sky; they are like a drop of water in comparison with a great ocean.

What Zen is here warning against is the danger, into which millions of scriptural fundamentalists throughout the major theistic religions have fallen, of mistaking the pipeline for the source. Scriptural texts, Zen teaches, are channels – some more clogged than others – of religious ideas, nothing more; to think of them otherwise is to fall into idolatry (and perhaps atheism, since it implies a refusal to love God with all one's mind). It is, according to an ancient Zen story, as if a man were pointing at the moon and asks his friend 'What is that?', to which he receives the reply, 'That's your finger.' John Wesley described himself as 'a man of one book' (the Bible); a Zen Master would have told him to throw it away. The point always to bear in mind when reflecting on Zen is its emphasis on living intuitively – hitting the target without taking aim, which could hardly occur if at every stage the archer were consulting his instruction manual in order to be certain of what the aim should be.

The lumber which for Zen is the most obstructive impediment on the path to satori is intellectual and doctrinal debate. About this, masters warned from generation to generation. Mumon, for instance (14, 19), recounted a discussion between Nansen Fugan, an earlier master (748–835), with his student and successor Joshu Jushin (778–897):

> Joshu asked Nansen, 'What is the Way?' Nansen said, 'Everyday life is the Way.' Joshu asked: 'Can it be studied?' Nansen replied: 'If you try to study it, you will be far away from it.' Joshu persisted: 'How can I know the Way, if I do not study it?' Nansen replied: 'The Way is not a matter of knowing or not knowing. Knowing is confusion; not knowing is delusion. When you have truly reached the Way, you will be in no doubt; you will find the Way as vast and boundless as the sky. You cannot call the Way either good or bad.

Hui-neng, a century earlier, had developed the argument quoted on p. 67.

> Religious doctrines are unimportant; so disputes on doctrinal matters should be shunned . . . Those who think that perfect wisdom can be realised by believing certain doctrines, will never realise perfect wisdom.

How grim in comparison seems Gerontius's desperate expression in *The Dream* of a 'true' belief in the creeds, in order to gain his way into heaven. His submissive resignation, allied with his terror, are, as Nietzsche pronounced, two of the curses of theism.

To cause the human mind to stop thinking is, of course, almost as impossible a task as stopping the lungs from breathing. Nevertheless, it can be achieved, as countless zen teachers and masters over the centuries testify. In the Rinzai school, one of the two main schools in Japan, those seeking to engage themselves in zazen were given a helping hand through the use of the *koan*, a statement or question to which there can be no logical response. The words are framed to form a paradox, meaning, etymologically, 'beyond thinking' (Greek *para* = beyond, *dokein* = to think). In one usage the word refers to strange, virtually self-contradictory statements or situations, such as the call to mobilise for peace, or the description of religion as trying to satisfy man through its essential purpose which is to make him dissatisfied. A second kind of paradox is one in which impossible terms are imposed on real-life circumstances, such as the call to pull oneself up by one's own bootstraps, or to roll a stone uphill by the use of gravity. It is this type of paradox that zen developed into the koan, and today there are thousands in circulation. A koan is not a riddle, and is therefore unsolvable by logical, rational thinking. Instead, it requires a transition to another level of comprehension. That is, the student is taught that his intellect will not help, and that it is useless to look for precedents in reaching a response. Rather, he must make an intuitive leap, taking him into a world beyond logical and dualistic distinctions. Frequently, the koan is used in a *mondo*, or question-and-answer session between a zen master and his pupil. The two most famous and widely used collections of koans are the 'Pi-yen-lu', literally the 'Bluegreen Cliff Record', dating from the twelfth century; and the 'Wumen men-kuan', literally the 'Gateless Gate', (*wu* is Chinese for satori) from the thirteenth. A koan from this later collection, is the 'Chao-chou, Dog':

> A monk once asked Master Chao-chou: 'Does a dog really have Buddha-nature or not?'
> Chau-chou said, '*Wu*' (in Japanese, *Mu*).

'*Wu*' is known as the *wato*, or punch-line, to which, or to several of which, all koans lead. Zen masters recognised the danger of a student's learning ancient koans and answering by rote, thus doing the reverse of what the exercise was aiming to bring about; one Master, in fact, had all copies of the 'Pi-yen-lu' burned in his monastery, so that the student had to make his own intuitive leap. It should be emphasised that the use of the koan is a feature only in the Rinzai school. In the Soto school, the second surviving school in Japan today, no words are allowed for those engaging in zazen: the original Bodhidharma tradition of simply facing a wall is continued, with no aid except that which originates within the meditator, sitting in silence.

Intuitive leaps do not come easily to those who have been raised to believe that the rational human mind, and the intellectual explorations in which it engages itself, are the crown of nature. Yet Zen, many of whose teachers have been scholars of distinction, is unyielding in its assertion that to gain spiritual enlightenment one must reach beyond reason. One master, for instance, when asked why Bodhidharma had left India for China in the first place, replied, 'The oak tree in the garden.' How far anyone can 'see' the point of that reply will indicate the extent of his or her journey along the path of Zen.

Zen teaching appropriates the Hindu image of the mountain which, it states, all human beings are climbing, and gives it a distinctive slant. In Hindu teaching, the image shows many paths, some broad, some narrow, threading their way to the mountain top. Whichever route they take, Hinduism teaches, all who seek enlightenment are making for the same goal, and all will finally achieve it. Zen accepts that there are many routes up the mountain, but adds the distinctive rider that, on whichever track a Zen practitioner begins, he must eventually branch off on his own. He will not reach the top of the mountain on others' shoulders, even though they may carry him for part of the way. 'If you search for the void, you can never reach it,' says one koan; and, using a different image: 'If you run away from the void, you can never be free of it.' Thus, by trusting solely to insights discovered by others, it will be impossible to make that final intuitive leap without which satori is impossible; and the leap takes place spontaneously and without forethought.

It may be argued that Zen has removed itself so far from the original Buddhist teaching as contained in the tripitaka, the 'three baskets' of the *Pali Canon* (the Dharmapada), that it is difficult to categorise its teaching within the Buddhist confines and so should be designated simply as 'Zen' without the added restrictive 'Buddhism'. This seems a reasonable argument; in fact, as we shall see in the next chapter, Zen has more in common with its fellow philosophy in China, Taoism, than it has with the other expressions of Mahayana Buddhism, with which it is usually linked. In fact, its teaching that enlightenment must be sought by the individual's following his or her own path has the paradoxical effect of, on the one hand, separating itself from all other religions and, on the other, connecting it with them all. Its individuality, its emphasis on personal autonomy, and its demand for authenticity on the part of all who follow the way to satori, link it closely with existentialism, especially as expressed by Kierkegaard and Nietzsche, both of whom, in their different ways, had experience of the 'leap in the dark'. But at the same time, members of most of the world's religions have sensed that Zen teachers are making explicit what is implicit, if often unexpressed, in their own religion. Michael Diener, the Japanologist, describes it (*EPR 443* – see bibliography) in these terms:

(Zen) expresses the primordial perfection of everything existing . . . designated by the most various names, experienced by all the great saints, sages, and founders of religions of all cultures and times.

But Zen is not simply for the founders or exceptional figures of the world's religions: it is available to all, of whatever religion or none. Diener boldly comments:

It is the immediate expression and actualisation of the perfection which is present in every person and at every moment.

In Zen, as in Theravada Buddhism, there is no God; yet the quest for satori could be described as nothing other than a religious quest, and the seated meditation which is zazen can be described only as a religious activity. And the goal is available to all who sense that life is more than merely the embrace of material values, and a person more than a physical body. Zen, like its partner in China, Taoism, expresses metaphysics without theology.

One feature of Zen which links it with a central aspect of Taoism may be mentioned before we turn specifically to Lao Tzu and the *Tao Te Ching*. This is the *haiku*: a short poem of seventeen syllables, in which is expressed a sense of mystery, usually linked with man's experience of nature. Like Zen teaching in general, it leaves much more unsaid than explicitly stated; and like Zen, it appeals to the intuition, not to any kind of formal analysis. The essence of a haiku, like that of a Zen garden or a Zen house, is its simplicity; yet, as always in Eastern writings, simplicity means not stupidity (as in 'simple Simon'), but directness and profundity. Its Nature-mysticism involves a sense of unity between *Homo sapiens* and the natural world which is the basic context of his living; and beyond this form of mysticism, it expresses a unity with what Ninian Smart (*The Religious Experience of Mankind* p. 231) has termed 'the divine Emptiness which suffuses the world of phenomena'. The haiku expresses this mystery through a particular image or individual event. The following examples are translated by Alan Watts in *The Way of Zen* (pp. 186–7, quoted in Smart. op. cit.). Being translations, the original seventeen syllables of each poem have been lost, but the essence of the poems remains:

In the dark forest
   A berry drops:
      The sound of water.

The dewdrop world –
   It may be a dewdrop,
      And yet – and yet –

The sea darkens;
   The voices of the wild ducks
      Are faintly white.

The woodpecker
   Keeps on in the same place:
      Day is closing.

It is difficult to conclude that the condition evoked by any one of these haikus, especially when reflection on them is more than cursory, together with the feelings which may well be inspired by such ponderings, are anything other than a religious experience, opening the way to satori, suuyata, the void.

Note

1. For further details of this and other basic Buddhist teaching see my *Understanding Eastern Philosophy*.

Chapter 8

Taoism

The Tao is like a well: used but never used up.
It is like the eternal void: filled with infinite possibilities.
It is hidden but always present.
I do not know who gave it birth.
It is older than God.

(*Tao Te Ching*, 4, trans. S. Mitchell)

Taoism stands alongside Confucianism and Buddhism as one of the three philosophies/religions which have stamped Chinese thought and culture over the past two and a half millennia. When Bodhidharma brought Ch'an (Zen) Buddhism to China around the sixth century CE, he found that the ground had been well prepared by Taoist teachers to receive the message he brought, and throughout subsequent centuries the two schools have not found it difficult to function harmoniously alongside each other.

Although in general the Chinese, like the teachers of India, do not make as clear-cut a distinction between philosophy and religion as we do in the West, with our stronger analytical traditions, Taoism does in fact fork unambiguously in two directions: *Tao-chia*, philosophical Taoism; and *Tao-chiao*, religious Taoism, though the latter is often translated as magical Taoism. Our main concern is with Tao-chia, but, since Tao-chiao has always been its most popular expression (and is so even in the British Taoist Society), we should not overlook it.

Its basic aim is the attainment of immortality, and religious Taoists designate their great teachers of the past as 'immortals' (*hsien*), whom they believe to be still among us in one guise or another. The immortals are often depicted in Chinese art as covered with feathers, symbolising their rising and ascension into the air to the highest stages of self-realisation. W. Bauer (*China und die Hoffnung auf Gluck*, 1974 p. 157) draws on this description of them by a fourth-century Taoist scholar, Ko Hung:

Some immortals ascend to the clouds, their body upright, and they fly among the clouds without beating of wings; some glide across the cloudy vapour by harnessing a dragon and ascend up to the very steps of Heaven . . . Their kind has attained an eternal life, free from death; but before they reach their goal they have to shed all human emotions and all ambitions about fame and glory . . . They have abandoned their former nature and are pervaded by a new life energy.

There are, according to Tao-chiao, a number of ways to achieving the status of a hsien. These include: first, various alchemic practices, the most powerful of which involves the use of cinnabar, sulphide of mercury, symbolising what Philip Rawson (*Tao*, p. 263) termed the 'nuclear energy of joined yin and yang' (though there is a cautionary tale here, as many Chinese went beyond the symbolic to the literal use of cinnabar, and died from mercury poisoning after consuming it – the ultimate in irony for anyone seeking longevity); second, embryonic breathing (*hsing-ch'i*) and other exercises to stretch the body and allow the breath to circulate more freely (Tao-yin), a much more intense and prolonged process than *pranayama*, the rhythmic control of the breath practised in yoga; third, meditation, especially the form which is becoming increasingly popular in the West, T'ai chi chu'an, whereby the practitioner seeks to align his or her body, through subtle and graceful movements, with the natural, though invisible, energies of the locality; and fourth, certain sexual practices (*fang-chung shu*), during which it is believed that the male yang is nourished by the female yin, and vice versa, thus mirroring the marriage of the masculine heaven with the feminine earth which, they believed, brought all things into being. As in both Hindu and Tibetan Buddhist Tantrism, though with a different aim in mind, the physical act of sex, particularly the exchange of bodily fluids, was viewed as a supremely efficacious way of bringing about longevity.

All these practices had, it was believed, one virtue in common: they enabled the practitioner to extend his or her life-span, and possibly become an immortal. What this essentially required was harmony with the *Ch'i*, and for an understanding of this concept we must turn to Tao-chia.

Philosophical Taoism is concerned not with longevity, but with the achievement and enjoyment of the eternal here and now; and here the link with Ch'an (Zen) Buddhism in unambiguous. Both Tao-chia and Ch'an teach the virtues of simplicity, naturalness, and the discovery of the intuitive side of one's nature. However, whereas teachers of Ch'an exhort followers of its path to turn away from the tangible world, a process exemplified by Bodhidharma's 'nine years facing the wall', Taoism encourages its followers to discover the intuitive side of their natures by enjoying the natural world around them so as to experience a harmony with it that is beyond self-consciousness. Once again we have encountered the advocacy of mysticism, but in Taoism there is an important and unique emphasis: the key is to be *natural*.

When you are content to be simply yourself
and don't compare or compete,
everybody will respect you.

(*Tao Te Ching*, 8)

What, then, does 'Tao' mean? To be able to give a direct answer to this seemingly straightforward question would, paradoxically, be to fall into error, since, as the opening verse of the most famous of all Taoist classics states unambiguously,

The tao that can be told is not the eternal Tao;
The name that can be named is not the eternal Name.

This couplet is from the *Tao Te Ching*, the 'classic of the way and its power'. According to Chinese tradition, it was written by Lao Tzu, a famous teacher and mystic of the sixth century BCE, just before he removed himself from civilisation in order to become a recluse. It is now generally agreed by sinologists that the work is the product of many hands (Lao Tzu means 'great master', which is more a title than a name); that it was compiled over some centuries; and was finalised in its present form around the second century BCE.

According to the *Tao Te Ching*, the Tao is *the first principle of the universe, the all-embracing reality from which everything else arises*. Although the Tao remains eternally unknowable, its power (Te) can enter into every human being, so that the test of one's commitment to Taoism is viewed as the extent to which one's life is in harmony with the Tao. (The Chinese hieroglyphic for 'philosophy' depicts a hand and a mouth, symbolising a condition where words are consistent with deeds.)

While one should be cautious about establishing cross-cultural likenesses, some commentators on Taoism have compared the concept of the Tao with that of Brahman in Hinduism. Brahman as the (unknown) ground of being certainly presents a parallel, but the immediacy of Brahman illustrated in the belief in the possibility of a union between it and the Atman is out of harmony with Taoist teaching, which accepts that, while a person may reflect the Tao in his or her life, nobody can possibly *know* the Tao. Other commentators, including George Chryssides (*Journal of Religious Studies* 19, pp. 1–11), find it not inapposite to view the Tao as having the same place in Taoist thought as the Godhead has in the thinking of (my example) Meister Eckhart: it is unknowable, but there could be nothing in the universe without its prevenient creative energy. This is a fair comment, but an important rider must be added: Taoism does not proceed to make any case for God, or gods, as divine powers operating under the Tao's auspices, so to speak. Section 42 of the *Tao Te Ching* puts the matter rather differently:

The Tao gives birth to One.
One gives birth to Two.
Two gives birth to Three.
Three gives birth to all things.

The 'One' to which the Tao gives birth – and was mentioned in relation to Tao-chiao – is Ch'i, or primordial breath (wind, spirit, energy, like the Hebrew word *Ruach* as used in Genesis 1: 2: 'The spirit of God moved upon the face of the waters'). It is the life-force that pervades and vitalises all things, the cosmic energy which brought the universe into being and continues to sustain it. Chryssides suggests that if the Tao is unknowable, Ch'i is the Tao that can be known – like God, the origin of all things even if, like God, it is not the unknown and unknowable origin of the origin. He argues that, while the Judaeo-Christian tradition certainly presents images of a 'hands-on' God, there are throughout their scriptures signs of development, leading, for example, to St John's link between Jesus, the Son of God, and the logos in Greek philosophy (John 1: 1 ff.). This is certainly a more advanced concept than that of a God who helps Adam to name the animals in the Garden of Eden, but it remains the case that the God who is involved with his people in all their doings is so fundamental to the theistic tradition that the idea of a 'Godhead' remains, at best, marginalised. The concept of the logos as defined in Greek thought is probably the nearest we have to that of the Tao outside China: but the concept must remain pure if the comparison is to be valid. To tinge it with Christian mythology, as in 'Son of God', is to undermine the comparison.

For Taoists even the Ch'i remains remote. It can be experienced, but only with time and dedication. If the Te, the power of the Tao in each individual life, is to be evinced, a force is needed which can be experienced more immediately. It is here that Taoists turn to the 'Two' to which the Ch'i gives birth. These are the twin forces of yin and yang, the polar opposites by which the universe functions, such as negative and positive, cold and heat, darkness and light, intuition and rationality, femininity and masculinity, earth and heaven. Neither of these can be without the other, and neither has any meaning without the other. We know the meaning of 'hot' only in relation to 'cold', of 'wet' to 'dry', of 'tall' to 'short', of 'dark' to 'light', of 'life' to 'death'. (We know that we are alive only because we know that we were once, and shall again be, dead. If we were eternal, there would be no word either for 'eternal' or for 'living'.)

These twin forces, the yin and the yang, operate throughout the world, giving us day and night, summer and winter, seedtime and harvest. As the symbol of yin and yang, the *T'ai-ch'i-tu* (diagram of the supreme ultimate) illustrates, there is, however, some light (yang) in the dark yin, and vice versa. This indicates two important features of life, which are often lost sight of. First, no living creature is entirely one or the other: there is some feminine yin in every male and some masculine yang in every female, and the wisest couple will recognise this and live together accordingly, with neither claiming to be the dominant partner (yang) in every aspect of their relationship. Second, and more importantly, neither yin nor yang is ever motionless; each is continuously moving into the other, which means that one must learn to recognise when to apply yin, and when yang, energies. This again means allowing the intuition to exert itself: to know when to speak out and when to remain quiet; when to be gentle and when to be violent; when to be active and when to stand and stare. Both the workaholic and the playboy are, according to the yin-yang doctrine, living distorted and incomplete lives because only half of their natures is being allowed expression. Neither the ant nor the grasshopper in Aesop's fable would receive Taoism's stamp of approval.

The 'Three' to which the Two give birth are heaven, earth and humanity. As we shall see, it is when there is harmony between these three – the yang of heaven, the yin of earth, and the human occupants of the arena which between them they bring into being – that the Te can be identified in people's lives. The final stage is the creation of 'all things' which we encounter and experience, for which 'the Three' are responsible.

The important consideration with Taoism, however, as with the concept of nirvana in Buddhism, is not to speculate on the meaning of the idea of the Tao, but to find out how to respond to its power (Te) in one's own life. The aim, as already mentioned, is to be natural, and the *Tao Te Ching* gives many hints about how this state may be achieved. One way is to practise *wu-wei*. This is often translated as living a life of 'non-action', but a more accurate translation would be not to take any *inappropriate* action. The most famous exponent of Taoism who was unquestionably a historical figure was the teacher of the third century BCE, Chuang-Tzu (Master Chuang). He argued that many of the things we do and the words we speak are simply a waste of time and breath, since the situation we are discussing or trying to affect cannot be changed by our efforts: all we're actually doing, he said, was 'flaying the air'. Or worse: our frenetic efforts may actually lead to the loss of what was wholesome and acceptable in itself. We destroy a lily by gilding it; a snake is no longer a snake if we paint legs on it; we shall not help young wheat to grow by tugging at it. We must practise patience and learn how, in the words of the religious existentialist Tillich, 'to read the signs of the times', acting only at the right time and with the minimum amount of effort. In fact, if we learn how to wait, we shall frequently find that no action is necessary in any case. The *Tao Te Ching* (15) states:

> Do you have the patience to wait
> till your mud settles and the water is clear?
> Can you remain unmoving
> till the right action arises by itself?

There is a skill involved in such behaviour, which few people raised in Western cultures have learned (and perhaps not many modern Chinese: although Confucianism has been restored in their school syllabuses, Taoism has no place). A Western equivalent might be, 'Never do today what you can possibly leave till tomorrow', where the operative word is *possibly*. It sounds like a policy of procrastination, and therefore heinous, and is condemned in the German couplet, 'Morgen, Morgen, nur nicht heute / Sagen alle faule Leute' ('Tomorrow, tomorrow, anything but today / That's what lazy people say'). This may be the case; but it may also be the case that a person recognises what is essential to be completed today and what can preferably be left till later, bearing in mind that, when it is later, the job may no longer be necessary. Chuang-Tzu was, in fact, active in public life and must have been widely respected since he was offered the prime ministership of his province. Wu-wei means striking only when the iron is hot, sowing one's seed – whether in deed or word – and leaving it time to burgeon. Where disagreement with another person occurs, its approach is to present one's viewpoint unambiguously, then leave it time to germinate – if there is any worth in the idea – in the mind of the other, rather than to overcome the other with decibels or, worse, to force him to accept a viewpoint or an activity against either his will or his personal assessment of the situation. Wu-wei is the way of the diplomat, not the dictator; of the philosopher, not the proselytiser.

Another concept in Taoism with which wu-wei is linked is *fu*, meaning 'returning'. This could be interpreted as aligning oneself with the yin and yang by understanding that seasons, whether in nature or in a nation's culture and values, arrive and pass, only to return again and pass away again, so that the wise person will accommodate his living to the eternal process of change. More basically Taoist is the concept of fu as returning, or, at any rate, remaining loyal, to one's roots:

> If you let yourself be blown to and fro,
> you lose touch with your root.
> If you let restlessness move you,
> you lose touch with who you are.

(op. cit., 26)

Fu is one example among many in Eastern philosophy of an idea which is mirrored in existentialist thought, with its emphases on, for example, authenticity, avoiding bad faith, even autonomy. (See my *East of Existentialism*.)

The same is true of another Taoist virtue which reflects but antecedes Zen. This is *p'u*, literally an unhewn block, and is an image used to denote simplicity, even innocence: not arising from ignorance, but from a backcloth of full awareness of the human condition: childlikeness without being childish. It means being oneself, avoiding what Sartre was to term 'bad faith' or living behind a mask. To live according to p'u is to speak as one feels, to behave according to the person one is, or has become; in other words, to act naturally. The *Tao Te Ching* (25) states:

Man follows the earth.
Earth follows the universe.
The universe follows the Tao.
The Tao follows only itself.

That final phrase has also been translated as 'suchness', the spontaneous and intuitive state of *tzu-yan*, meaning 'being such of itself', 'being natural'. In human beings, it includes everything which is free of human intention or external influences: that which is in harmony with itself. It may therefore be linked with wu-wei with its call for action only when it is appropriate – that is, when it is the natural action for those particular circumstances. When a person achieves this condition (which is not easy), he or she can be described as being at one with the Tao. It will not be achieved by academic research, or the study of sacred texts, or through a correct observance of ritual: like Zen, Taoism relegates all these activities to a low ranking on the scale of spiritual aids. It will be gained by living one's life in accordance with the natural forces of the universe, expressed both in nature itself and in human nature. As one of the contributors to G. Beky's *Die Welt des Tao* ('The World of Tao'), Akira Ohaima, states (p. 126):

The Tao acts like an immanent energy, a mysterious presence within the world of the ten thousand things. Therefore the individual effects of the ten thousand things – if they are not prevented from following their own nature – are in accordance with the *tzu-jan* [tsu-yan] of the Tao. What matters is not the self-conscious intentional striving for oneness with the Tao, but rather the fact that human action is identical with the Tao that is present and acting in man. That is *tzu-jan*.

While there are parallels between Taoism and Indian thought, it is important to recognise its distinctiveness, especially because of issues raised in Chapter 9. One could call the Tao the 'ground of being'; but unlike the Hindu view of Brahman, which can be known through being awakened to the Atman, the Tao must be preceded, tacitly at least, by the epithet 'unknowable': which implies that there really is no counterpart. The Zen experience of satori, entry into the void, is probably closer to Taoist ontology, but there remains a difference between Taoism and Zen in relation to the world, the 'ten thousand things'. Zen can be compared with Taoism in its treatment of the natural world as a mystery, which emerges through the haiku (and sometimes in a koan); and Chinese rural paintings often create the same sense of mystery in the presence of something awesome and inexplicable. Both encourage an intuitive approach to nature, which results in a sense of deep respect for that with which we should always be co-operating rather than exploiting. For Taoism, however, (and in this it exemplifies one of the major differences between Indian and Chinese philosophy) this is enough: to be at one with nature is a sign of being in harmony with the Tao. I shall discuss shortly the significance of this oneness with reference to Taoist art, but it is immediately clear that we are here engaged on a different quest from that followed by either Buddhists or Hindus. For them, while nature may be a valuable and often-sought context for enlightenment, it remains no more than that. The experience of moksha, or satori, are ultimately independent of anything which the tangible world provides, and can just as well be gained by facing a wall (though a Zen garden provides a context and can create a mood which is easily conducive to a spiritual experience). For Taoists, however, the relationship with nature is at the heart of the mystical experience, and this is illustrated continually in Taoist paintings.

The beauty of these paintings is being increasingly appreciated in the Western world, but it is not with their beauty alone that the artists have been concerned. Their primary purpose is to express Taoist values. The seventeenth-century painting by K'un-ts'an, *Among Green Mountains I build a House*, is typical, if not archetypical, and has countless imitators whose works today adorn living-room walls in Western homes. To begin with, there is a sense of deep tranquillity pervading the entire scene, providing the assurance of how easy it will be for anyone to be becalmed in such surroundings, and to share in its unhurried, if not entirely soundless, completeness. Then there is the sense of unity in the whole, with its various features blending into one another so that no one aspect protrudes. The river and its banks are at one with the trees alongside, and these in their turn harmonise with the mountain, so that its heights do not appear to impose on the valley below. Above all, the simply structured house merges with its natural surrounding – it could even be overlooked with a cursory glance – and the figure gazing from its unglazed window is not expressing ownership of what he surveys, but a reverence towards this manifestation of the Tao, of which he – or she – is privileged to be part. There is no sense of 'me', 'me', about either the house or its owner, any more than there is about the river, the trees, or the mountain. It is as far removed as one can imagine from the Western attitude to the natural world, as exemplified in the triumphalism of its newspapers after the first successful climbing of Mt Everest: 'Everest Conquered!' they proclaimed. A Taoist would see this attitude as typical human conceit, preferring to describe the event along the lines of permission to visit the mountain peak for a brief period before the guests scuttled off back down to the safety of the lower levels.

Equally important in the picture is the manifestation of the yin and the yang. As these move back and forth towards and away from each other, so we find a sense of movement between the various features. The yin of the river and the foliage merges with the yang of the trees and the mountain, while remaining distinctive entities in themselves. The yang sky and the yin earth are in partnership together, light and shade combine to give clarity and contrast. Yet overall there is, as in so many Taoist landscapes, a brooding sense of mystery. There is what Wordsworth described (and will be further discussed in Chapter 9) as 'a presence', a living spirit which pervades and unifies the whole, and with which the human participant is in communion. The mystery is given direct expression by the depiction of clouds and mist which pervade one side of the house. One senses that the hermit is experiencing an absorption in the whole which can be described only in mystical terms, on a par with the mysticism of Meister Eckhart and others of the theistic traditions; with the absorption of Atman and Brahman in the Hindu tradition; and the experience of the void, satori, in Zen. *Among Green Mountains I build a House* is, in fact and in short, a religious painting.

Even the food we eat can, as a balance of yin and yang, be evidence of this natural harmony and therefore a spiritual experience, and on this issue Taoism parts company with its Indian counterparts. While neither Hinduism nor Buddhism expresses the extreme suspicion of all foods as found in the Jainite tradition (because for them eating means the expression of *ahimsa*, violence, towards living entities and is therefore detrimental to the spiritual quest), there remains the whiff of self-denial in all their different schools. The view frequently propounded in both Hinduism and Buddhism is that, on the whole, abstinence is more spiritually beneficial than indulgence (and this applies to sex as well as food). This is a moot point, of course, but most Taoists would view this attitude as a straightforward example of acting unnaturally.

Taoists seek enlightenment through what heaven and earth provide, rejoicing in their glories and discovering through them the deepest mysteries of the universe. So it is seen as unnatural to deny oneself that which is both health-giving and enjoyable; in fact, anyone who knows how to balance his diet is at one with the Tao, so that a chef could well be described as the Chinese equivalent of the Hindu guru.

Taoism's ideal is to balance yin and yang forces, an aim which is expressed in the teachings of Confucius, who was – and still is – often viewed as a rival to the Taoists, but saw himself as one who was seeking to apply their ideas and ideals in the practical world of family, social and political life. He indicated, for example, how nations could experience the harmony of the Tao in the world of politics; his *Analects* reverberate with admonitions for rulers to rule with a light hand so that their subjects will not feel threatened or intimidated – and will thus be more co-operative with them in their enterprises.

Furthermore, and coming closer to home than politics, Taoism reaches out into regions which Hindu mystics leave virtually unexplored – the sexual harmony between a man and a woman, when give and take, assertion and submission, hardness and softness, fierceness and tenderness, mirror the yin-yang forces, the twin pillars of the Ch'i, the vital breath by which the Tao is

known. Much Taoist art, whether paintings or other artifices, features the yin
and yang in openly sexual terms, abounding with images of male and female
genitalia expressed not only in scenes of human sexuality, but as images in
stones, fruits, plants, or any other natural object which resembles a vulva or
a lingam. A mutually fulfilling sex life is viewed as a sign that those concerned
have discovered the harmony and completion of the yin and yang, and so are
sharing what may be without apology called a religious experience.

Western attitudes on this matter have been sadly distorted, perhaps ter-
minally, by the fear of sex which runs virtually unmodified throughout
Christian scriptures and traditions. It is still expressed in high places, as is
exemplified by a member of the British Upper House who objected to sex
education in schools on the grounds that it 'gave children wrong ideas'. Ray
Monk records in his *Ludwig Wittgenstein* that the philosopher's friend and
disciple, Maurice Drury, expressed disgust over the bas-relief on the wall of
one of the Luxor temples which depicted the god Horus with an erect phal-
lus in the act of ejaculating and collecting the semen in a bowl. Wittgenstein
rejected Drury's disapproval:

> Why in the world shouldn't they have regarded with awe and reverence
> that act by which the human race is perpetuated? Not every religion has
> to have St Augustine's attitude to sex.
>
> (op. cit., p. 454)

(For further reflections on this theme, see Chang's *The Tao of Love and Sex*.)

The harmony of the Tao, then, is seen as reflected in a healthy body, a
reciprocal relationship, a fine balance of work and leisure, of committed
time and spare time. A Taoist's diary will have enough engagements to
fulfil the yang side of his life with enough free time not to leave the yin
incomplete. Both the lack of responsible commitment reflected in an empty
diary, and the furious round of unsatisfactorily completed duties in one
that is overcrowded, would be viewed as unlikely to lead its owner into the
joy of being at ease with himself, an ease which is one of the sure indica-
tors of being in harmony with the Tao, and possessing the Te. The *Tao Te
Ching*, 27 states:

> A good traveller has no fixed plans
> and is not intent upon arriving.
> A good artist lets his intuition
> lead him wherever it wants.
> A good scientist has freed his mind of concepts
> and keeps his mind open to what is.
>
> Thus the Master is available to all people
> and doesn't reject anyone.

He is ready to use all situations
and doesn't waste anything.
This is called embodying the light.

In the Taizé Community in France, this virtue is described as being *disponible* – available. I should describe it also as being religious, which leads to our final consideration.

To the untutored mind, Taoism may well appear to be a philosophy of life rather than a religion. It makes no distinction between the sacred and the secular, has no dedicated buildings, no liturgy, no holy books, no moral code except to be natural, no forms of prayer and, above all, no God in any sense in which that concept is expressed in other religions. While Tao-chiao, religious Taoism, aims for longevity in this life, it affirms no belief in a life beyond and has no conception of reincarnation. To be sure, Chuang-Tzu, who evinced no signs of mourning after the death of his beloved wife, said to his critics:

> How do I know that loving life is not a delusion? How do I know that in hating death, I am not like a man who, having left home in his youth, has forgotten the way back?

But this was a cryptic question rather than an affirmation of belief, on a par with the anti-anthropomorphism of his famous remark after dreaming that he was a butterfly:

> Now I don't know whether I'm a man dreaming he is a butterfly, or a butterfly dreaming it is a man.

As mentioned on p. 13, Confucius – if we can take him according to his own self-description and number him among the Taoists – often referred to 'the way of heaven', but he used this phrase to mean no more than the ideal as we perceive it – the ideal way of ruling, of relating to other people, of achieving fulfilment. He was Nietzschean, in fact, in his insistence on being concerned with the problems of this world rather than using our energies preparing for the next. Asked about how we should serve the gods, he peremptorily replied that the service of our fellow men was enough of a challenge to anyone without wasting time on this vacuous consideration.

The *Tao Te Ching* is a more spiritual book than the writings of Confucius, but its reverence is certainly not directed towards any kind of divine architect or heavenly father, analogies which are typical in overtly religious organisations. In place of these it presents the natural world, the world of the 'ten thousand things', as both the context for living, and the catalyst of whatever philosophy we may embrace. To live naturally means to accept other people as, potentially at least, fellow-witnesses to the Tao, and consequently to accept them for their own sakes. This is the way of nature, with checks and balances which, on the whole, ensure that no single species plays too dominant a role. The wise person is therefore one who accepts his or her place in the natural order by co-operating with it, and so gaining the fulfilment of living in harmony with the Tao. It is pointless to try to alter or control nature: that is a form of megalomania which will bring inevitable disaster in one form or another – a disaster of the perpetrator's own making.

So the image we receive from the heart of Taoism is of a life lived without guile, without pretence, in tune with the natural forces of yin and yang, which are manifested in all that exists or occurs. The follower of what Alan Watts characterised in his translation of the *Tao Te Ching* as 'the Watercourse Way' learns how to adapt herself intuitively to any situation, to breathe in strength from what nature provides, so that, contented with her own self and with her role in life, she is able naturally to enrich the lives of those she encounters. According to the *Tao Te Ching*, this apparent ideal can become anyone's norm. If it means abandoning the rat race for a simpler way of living, then this is a change worth making, and many, in the West as well as in the East, are making that choice.

With this brief account of Taoism we reach the end of this overview of mysticism as experienced in selected religions of the world. It is difficult not to sympathise with Taoists' own assessment of their philosophy as one that, in its acknowledgement of an ultimate spiritual power which cannot be known or named, but is affirmed by the manifest world which we all encounter, is, in fact, a unifying factor between all religions. Confucians, Buddhists, Hindus, theists, have their own terms for the mystery, but in the end all are discussing the same thing. This may well be a valid assessment of Tao-chia; and if its religious or magical expression, Tao-chiao, remains fundamentally related to Chinese culture, even there (for example, in its forms of meditation) it may have a contribution to make in the quest for religion without God. The universal appeal of Taoism is expressed in an inscription on a Ming rock, dated 1556, and it sums up Taoism's central affirmation:

> Vast indeed is the Ultimate Tao,
> Spontaneously itself, apparently without acting,
> End of all ages and beginning of all ages,
> Existing before Earth and existing before Heaven,
> Silently embracing the whole of time,
> Continuing uninterrupted through all eons,
> In the East it taught Father Confucius,
> In the West it converted the 'Golden man' [the Buddha]
> Taken as pattern by a hundred kings,
> Transmitted by generations of sages,
> It is the ancestor of all doctrines,
> The mystery beyond all mysteries.

Chapter 9

Profane religion

> I heard flowers that sounded and saw notes that shone.
> (Saint-Martin, 'le philosophe inconnu': *L'Ésprit des choses*)

So far, this quest for religion has remained within the confines of established traditions in major world religions. We have designated the experiences of mystics within the theistic religions as expressive of religion at its highest level, that is, one in which God is either ignored or superseded in favour of the unknown and unknowable Godhead. In the religions of India we have identified peak experiences in which the participant either finds release from subjectiveness through absorption in the ground of being, as in Advaita Vedanta, or total loss of self in sunyata, the void, as in Theravada or Zen Buddhism. In China we have found in Taoism a religion which expresses oneness with the natural world, a unity which therefore brings about absorption of individual consciousness (the mystical experience) in a different context from that of Hinduism or Buddhism: one, in fact, which takes us a step closer to secular spirituality, a religious experience which does not look for any spiritual revelations or manifestations beyond those which the world constantly and naturally provides. In the teachings of Confucius, this rejection of 'another world' in favour of human relationships here and now, and of the cultivation of the (so-called) soul in favour of one's physical and mental needs, is given unambiguous expression.

This book is not, however, driven by any kind of proselytising zeal for these Eastern philosophies, whether theistic, non-theistic, or atheistic. Admittedly, it would harm nobody to spend some time practising yogic or Zen meditation, and it is hard to imagine any reader's life not being enriched through regular quiet reflections on the *Tao Te Ching* or Chuang Tzu (described ironically by Oscar Wilde when first translated into English in 1881 as 'a very dangerous book'). The purpose of this exploration is to indicate quite straightforwardly how all people can have religious experiences in familiar settings if they could simply open their eyes to the reality which surrounds them. That many eyes are not so opened is caused partly by obtuseness, but largely by the artificial separation of sacred from secular which, with rare exceptions, has dominated the teaching of religious institutions throughout their histories. As a result, it has become engrained in the human psyche that 'religion' involves certain specific acts, places, people, life-styles and beliefs, so that where these are absent from a person's life, he or she is generally viewed as not being religious. It is this assumption which must be refuted, as *inter alia*, A. N. Wilson (op. cit.) and Don Cupitt (op. cit.) have refuted it, Wilson on a classical/historical and Cupitt on a philosophical/aesthetic basis.

My intention is to direct the argument into the public arena in plainer and more direct terms than even these eminent writers – and others – have achieved. It seems to me beyond dispute that, on the one hand, religion is real and universal and, on the other, God is unreal but has localised aficionados. Only by accepting the second thesis can the first be established on a sure foundation. Religion and God must therefore go their separate ways. What this implies for the future of God-talk will be discussed in the final chapter. Here we shall pursue the first thesis and explore religion as a profane experience.

That word is not meant in its secondary sense of 'sullied' as in Shelley's lines:

> One word is too often profaned
> For me to profane it.

where he is accepting that the word 'love', used, as it is, in such a wide variety of contexts and with so many meanings, is inadequate to express his feelings. Rather, I am using the word in its original sense of *not being devoted to the sacred and the holy*, unconcerned with that which is formally and traditionally religious. It is illustrative of the main theme of this book that the primary meaning has led to the secondary: what is not holy has been charged by upkeepers of the holy as being defiled and debased, for the very reason that it is so separated. It is only one step further to speak of profane language, meaning that it is foul, abusive and vituperative. The greatest misunderstanding occurs when it is contrasted not only with 'holy', but also with 'spiritual', or even 'religious'. I wish to explore the concept somewhat along the lines of George Santayana's analysis:

> The *profane* poet is by instinct a naturalist. He loves landscape, he loves love, he loves the humour and pathos of earthly existence. But the religious prophet loves none of these things.

It may be mentioned *en passant* that 'profane' is not synonymous with 'secular', since that word implies that no viewpoint will be given serious consideration unless it can be justified on the basis of reason and evidence, a rationalistic approach to experience which is inessential, if not impossible, when reflecting on the sacred and profane. Here we are concerned with that facet of the human personality which we call intuition, subconscious perception, or what P. J. Thomajan described as 'a laconic apprehension of things seen and unseen'.

I wish, then, to extrapolate certain facets of human experience which have generally been accepted as profane in the sense that I have just outlined, but which are, in fact, channels of religion. The identifications which I am about to make may bemuse some of those who find fulfilment in one or other of these fields, but have never consciously thought of their experiences as religious. (For example, I put the point to Peter Blake apropos of painting, and he expressed total surprise that painting should be thought of in such terms.) What seems beyond question is that this lack of recognition stems not from any disagreement about the actuality of the experience in the artistic field, but from the custom or habit of associating religion only with typically religious contexts and language. To suggest, for example, that a great artist is the equivalent of a priest, a mediator of the divine, the transcendental, to those who are open to receive it, is to make a bolder claim than even many artists themselves have considered making. No matter: using Molière's description of the 'Médecin malgré lui' as an analogy, I am presenting the viewpoint that the contexts within which they work are religious contexts, and their activities, even if unacknowledged by themselves – 'despite themselves', as Molière expresses it – are those of people who in a different context would be described as holy.

The arts

The arena of fine arts – painting, music, literature, sculpture and so on – is universally acknowledged as the milieu *par excellence* of the human creative imagination. Unfortunately (or perhaps fortunately), it is notoriously difficult to state unambiguously what is meant by art. A common definition is 'the expression or pursuit of beauty'. This, as any student of aesthetics will be aware, begs many questions, with the key word 'beauty' vague in meaning. That need not be a deterrent to its use, however, as we saw when discussing the meaning of the word religion (Chapter 2). As Hospers pointed out (op. cit., pp. 67–77), vagueness is inevitable when trying to give a comprehensive definition of *anything*, however apparently uncomplicated and value-free (he gives the examples of 'game' and 'dog').

The question is whether the pursuit of beauty, the attempt to express the creative imagination in pictures, or sounds, or shapes, or words, is to be viewed as simply an expression of human ingenuity raised to its highest conceivable level, or as a communion with the divine, the eternal, the numinous as described on pp. 49–50. William Blake wrote:

> If the doors of perception were cleansed, everything would appear as it is, infinite.
>
> (*A Memorable Fancy*, pl. 14)

If that is the case, then Blake's younger contemporary Keats was not exaggerating when he closed his 'Ode on a Grecian Urn' with the couplet:

> 'Beauty is truth, truth beauty,' – that is all
> Ye know on earth, and all ye need to know.

Leaving aside any linguistic or conceptual analysis of this famous statement, its particularity is that it presents nothing less than a religious affirmation, with the denotation that the pursuit of beauty is a religious activity. As the material objects of water in baptism and bread and wine in Holy Communion are viewed by Christians as 'means of grace', so the oils and canvas of the painter, the stone of the sculptor, the words of the poet or novelist, the notes assembled by the composer, are the physical means whereby the numinous, the mystical, is conveyed. Commonplace objects thus become divine, the temporal is translated into the eternal, to the point of being realised as, in Michelangelo's words, 'a shadow of the divine perfection'.

While, then, the artist may in a sense be characterised as, 'a dreamer consenting to dream of the actual world' (Santayana), there is another, more far-reaching role of the artist, which is to enable people to share, if only partially, his or her vision of a dimension beyond this world of time and place. This was certainly how Beethoven viewed his music, as we saw on p. 16. His fundamentally materialistic and rationalistic philosophy prevented his finding refuge in a firm belief in personal immortality. In a letter to the painter Alexander Macco, he wrote:

> Continue to paint – and I shall continue to write down notes; and thus we shall live – for ever? – yes, perhaps, for ever.

But his friend Karl Peters assured him, in words quoted on p. 16, that he would be glorified as 'your music is religion'. It would be difficult to distinguish between the sense of the transcendental experienced during a performance of, say, his Seventh Symphony in a concert hall and the performance of High Mass in a cathedral – as difficult as it would be to distinguish between samadhi, the final 'limb' of the Hindu yogic path and that of satori in Zen Buddhism. All have – potentially at least – the effect of purifying and transforming the participant, so that he or she enters a different mode of being from the norm.

Music seems particularly empowered to bring this state about. There are, in fact, probably more people who experience the divine (even though they may not express it in such terms) through this medium than through any other. There are many who would find common ground with Goethe's assessment of Mozart as 'the human incarnation of the divine force of creation', as others would empathise with a similar description of Jesus, the second person of the Trinity. Music is the most direct of the arts, with no material object to create any kind of screen between artist and public; it does not raise its head at Sotheby's and make somebody a fortune as with paintings or, to a lesser degree, sculptures; it has no texts to lend themselves open to literary criticism, pitting the Leavis's with the C. S. Lewis's, the hierarchists with the universalists. *Cor ad cor loquitor* is, I find, truer of music than of any other art form, and, for many people, of anything else at all which they may encounter. The nineteenth-century Swiss philosopher and critic, Amiel, voiced his sense of the sublime in music when he wrote on a particular occasion of the 'indefinable power' which its sounds exerted over him:

> (The music) set me dreaming of another world, of infinite passion and supreme happiness . . . If music thus carries us to heaven, it is because music is harmony, harmony is perfection, perfection is our dream, and our dream is heaven.

Music has the unique power of enabling us to see visions and dream dreams, experiences which lie at the heart of religion. Heinrich Heine wrote of music as the religious mystics would have described their experiences of the divine. He described it as standing 'halfway between thought and phenomenon', and compared it with

> a sort of nebulous mediator, like and unlike each of the things it mediates – spirit that requires manifestation in time, and matter that can do without space.

In short, a mystery, as Heine concluded when he added:

> We do not know what music is.

So while, like nirvana in Buddhist thought, it is impossible to convey to another person either what music is or what its effects are on any particular listener, that person knows when something sublime has happened during the listening. Similarly, as Buddha said to a disciple who asked him about the nature of nirvana, 'When you enter into that state, you will know it for what it is.' To know something in this way, that is, within the depths of one's own being, may be beyond description, at least in any form of words which can be communicated to anyone else; but to be indescribable is not the same as to be unreal, as the study of phenomenology confirms.

This eulogy to music is not intended as a belittling of the other arts; indeed, there are many who experience the transcendental more readily through poetry, drama and other expressions of literature, others through the visual arts.

The feature common to all is their ability to bring about a state which Dietrich Bonhoeffer in one of his *Letters and Papers from Prison* described as 'the Beyond in the midst'. He was writing of a God who was no longer the remote God 'out there', but had become real at the heart of his being. It would be just as true so to describe the poet's muse. In his *A Defence of Poetry*, Shelley gave famous expression to this concept:

> [Poetry] is as it were the interpretation of a diviner nature through our own . . . It strips the veil of familiarity from the world, and lays bare the naked and sleeping beauty which is the spirit of its forms.

Though in a very different context, this is what Bonhoeffer was describing . Two millennia earlier, Plato had expressed the same thought:

> For all good poets, epic as well as lyric, compose their beautiful poems not by art, but because they are inspired and possessed . . . they are simply inspired to utter that to which the Muse impels them, and that only.

And through their inspiration, akin to that of prophets and priests, seers and saints, others can share, if only in part, the transcendental, mystical experience to which they bear witness.

The painter takes his place among the writers and musicians. We saw in the last chapter how Taoists turn to their brushes in order to express the Tao, 'the mystery beyond all mysteries', on the paper before them, illustrating the presence of the Te, the power of the Tao, in the world around: again, the beyond in the midst. These paintings were, in fact, felt by many who produced them to be more effective in conveying the mystery than, in the words of Laurence Binyon (*Painting in the Far East*):

> the gross impediments of complex matter allow to be transmitted to our senses in the visible world around us. A picture is seen as a sort of apparition from a more real world of essential life.

This point would probably be challenged by some lovers of nature but, as I tried to describe on pp. 86–7, it is impossible not to be drawn into the haunting sense of mystery created by these Chinese artists. Don Cupitt gives frequent testimony to the power of Chinese painting, but does not confine to Eastern painters alone the ability of this medium to bring viewers to a feeling of religion. In fact, he has affirmed that there is more religion in art, abstract art in particular, than there is in theology (see *After God*, pp. 118 ff.).

It may be argued that the examples of the arts which I have selected are from the 'top drawer', and that most people's efforts in this field belong somewhat lower down. For every painting worthy of the name there are a thousand daubs, for every poem, a world of doggerel, for every novel on the shelves, a myriad of scribblings scattered around floors or under the bed. Are all these creations to be hailed as channels of the divine?

This is not the place to enter the vexed debate about the validity of any kind of hierarchical structure among artists. There are voices raised in defence of the view that all productions in this field are works of art, the local poetry circle's efforts as much as those of Shakespeare or Milton, the primary school's modelling class a scene of creative activity as much as one conducted by Michaelangelo, the paintings of those attending the local institute as much as those of Rembrandt or Picasso. Whatever one's assessment of these works, it can be affirmed that the process of producing them, by the enthusiast, the student, or the child, may be as creative to that person as is the pursuit of the Muse to an acknowledged poet. Anyone engaged in the act of painting could be involved in a religious experience. The fact that not all works of art are equally absorbing to the listener, the viewer or the reader is no obstacle to my argument. After all, even those who seek a religious experience solely in traditional religious contexts will acknowledge that by no means all occasions bring about the sense of the numinous. For every glorious High Mass or Morning Prayer there are humdrum occasions when it seems that the motions alone are being gone through, the officiant apparently trying to remember whether he locked his car; and for every inspirational sermon there are a score which suggest that the dry rot is not only in the woodwork.

What will be attested unambiguously is the power of the arts to take people out of 'our bourne of time and place', as Tennyson expressed our everyday condition, into the eternal, where time and place are no more. Millions will confirm that during the performance of a particular play, or piece of music, or when gazing at some painting, they become absorbed in the work to the extent that all temporal and spacial awareness evaporates, suggesting that they have for an indeterminate period moved from (or blotted out) that part of the brain which contains consciousness of this awareness. It would, in fact, be impossible for the individual emerging from such a state of absorption to say with confidence how long he or she had been in this condition – one which can be described only as a transcendental state. It is difficult to avoid the conclusion that such moments, in the context of the arts, are as validly mystical, as spiritually beneficial, as anything experienced within traditional religious contexts. They are all, in fact, religious experiences, expressions of Adi Shankara's Fourth State, of Zen satori, of samadhi in both Hindu and Buddhist meditation. And one common feature of them all is that there is no reference to God.

Nature

Since Adam and Eve were first tempted to eat an apple from a tree in the
Garden of Eden, nature has been the continuous backcloth to human activity. It has shaped lives by providing the ceaseless round of change, through
seedtime to flowering, harvest to apparent decay: but only apparent,
because underlying the seeming death of winter, the forces are preparing for
the inevitable further seedtime which follows. On this stage, all human
virtues and vices have had a part to play, values and priorities established,
life-changing decisions made, life created and life destroyed. Without
nature – and this is not merely because of the evolutionary process: it
would be just as much the case if the creationist theory were found to be
true – there would be no human existence as we have known it. It deter-
mines the air we breathe, the food we eat, even the clothes we wear and the
buildings we inhabit. By extension, it affects how we spend our time, our
abilities and our money. Our planet is a living organism because of nature;
to be deprived of it would mean passing our time of existence on a dead
sphere.

Few will disagree with this assessment, even those urban dwellers who
have never seen a live cow, a hedgerow in bloom, or an apple orchard in
flower. Where disagreement has arisen has been about the model or combination of models by which one should interpret nature. Over the centuries,
these have varied enormously. The Judaeo-Christian-Islamic tradition views
nature as subservient to *Homo sapiens*, who is given lordship over it. In the
past, it was viewed, alongside their scriptures, their religious authorities, and
their consciences, as one of the four means whereby God's will could be
made known. Leibniz, in his *Principles of Nature and of Grace, Founded on
Reason*, wrote:

> It follows from the supreme perfection of God that in producing the uni-
> verse He chose the best possible plan, containing the greatest variety
> together with the greatest order, the best arranged situation, place, and
> time; the greatest effect produced by the simplest means; the most power,
> the most knowledge, the most happiness and good in created things of
> which the universe admitted . . . the result of all these claims must be the
> most perfect actual world that is possible. Otherwise it would not be
> possible to explain why things have happened as they have rather than
> otherwise.

This is the view of nature reflected in the hymn 'All things bright and
beautiful . . . the Lord God made them all.' (It was mocked by Voltaire in
Candide with the sardonic comment, 'All is for the best in the best of all
possible worlds.') The nemesis of this idealistic model arrived with
Darwin, the teaching of evolution, the realisation of how prodigal nature

is in its reproductive processes, and its total indifference to the destruction that may be caused as, for instance, only one sea tortoise in a thousand, born in the sand along the seashore, survives to take up its natural existence in the sea. This indifferent profligacy led to Tennyson's disenchantment with nature as he had earlier viewed it (expressed, for instance, in his poem 'Maud') and his subsequent view of it expressed in *In Memoriam*, LVI:

> Man . . .
> Who trusted God was love indeed,
> And love Creation's final law –
> Though Nature, red in tooth and claw
> With ravine, shriek'd against his creed.

However, our enquiry is not into the ethics of nature (there are none, since nature follows its own path, as water falls and stones crush). It is its mystical aspect which is our present concern, and those who have so experienced it have been untroubled by its indifference to what among human beings are crucial issues – right and wrong, good and bad. Those who experience nature's inherent mysticism have not fretted themselves about the fact that the field which seems so tranquil on a summer's day (or in the dead of winter) is the slaughterhouse for a million insects; that the ivy which looks beautiful surrounding a tree is, in fact, stifling it; or that the sole purpose of the birds hopping about in the garden is to fill their bellies. It is not the detail but rather nature as a living entity, a unity, with which they are concerned, characterised by Isaac Newton (*Opticks*, III, i) as that which 'is very consonant and conformable with herself'. This is nature without purposiveness, except that of 'to be'; nature in harmony with itself, constantly destroying and recreating in the wholeness of its being; the nature of which Goethe wrote:

> Each of her works has an essence of its own; each of her phenomena a special characterisation; and yet their diversity is in unity.
>
> (Huxley, 1869)

It has, in other words, the power to remove us from the haven – and the limitations – of the here and now into the fathomless pool of the subconscious, where time and place are no more, the distant past is now, and the far away is here. In those moments we experience eternity and omnipresence, kindled by the wisdom of the ages. Then, all that can be attributed to divinity is ours: we join the mystics past and present in affirming with an unshakeable certainty, *tat tvam asi*. This is enlightenment; this is true knowledge; this is religion. It is the dream time of the aborigine, samadhi of the yogin, the Buddhist's nirvana, the void, the Zen satori, and the beatific vision of the western mystics. Blake, in his 'Auguries of Innocence', gives felicitous expression to this vision in words to which every schoolchild should be introduced while the sense of wonder remains:

> To see a World in a grain of sand,
> And a Heaven in a wild flower,
> Hold Infinity in the palm of your hand,
> And Eternity in an hour . . .

And to those who cannot recognise this numinous element in the natural world his subsequent admonition may apply:

> He who doubts from what he sees
> Will ne'er believe, do what you please.
> If the Sun and Moon should doubt,
> They'd immediately go out.

Aurobindo Ghose, in his *Essays on the Gita* 2,1,9 (1920), argues that nature can only be a partial manifestation of the Godhead which is infinitely greater than anything which can be apprehended here and now. He states:

> By his very infinity, by his absolute freedom, he exists beyond all possibility of integral formulation in any scheme of worlds or extension of cosmic Nature, however wide, complex, endlessly varied this and every world may seem to us.

This is effectively confirming that the Tao that can be talked about, or experienced when in tune with nature, is not the eternal Tao, a sentiment with which I have already concurred. But Taoism proceeds with the affirmation that we *can* experience the Te, the power or spirit of the Tao, in our lives and that one indication that we have achieved this is a sense of deep harmony with nature. It is, in fact, difficult to avoid the conclusion that on this matter Taoism offers greater insight than Hinduism. It indicates how arenas which present themselves to us here and now can enable us to achieve spiritually all that is, in fact, possible here and now. Since we cannot know the Godhead or the Tao, our religious experience must be through what we can know. To requote Keats's words: 'This is all Ye know on earth, and all ye need to know.'

This knowledge is expressed unambiguously in words to which I referred earlier, Wordsworth's 'Lines composed a few miles above Tintern Abbey': a poem about nature with which, as a resident of Tintern, I can readily empathise; but, much more, a deeply religious poem, as these words illustrate:

> And I have felt
> A presence that disturbs me with the joy
> Of elevated thoughts; a sense sublime
> Of something far more deeply interfused,
> Whose dwelling is the light of setting suns,
> And the round ocean, and the living air,
> And the blue sky, and in the mind of man;
> A motion and a spirit, that impels
> All thinking things, all objects of all thought,
> And rolls through all things. Therefore am I still . . .
> . . . well pleased to recognise
> In nature and the language of the sense,
> The anchor of my purest thoughts, the nurse,
> The guide, the guardian of my heart, and soul
> Of all my moral being.

Here are words, to quote their author out of context, 'too deep for tears'. I have found no deeper expression of the religious experience anywhere in the world's sacred literature. It is significant that on the BBC Radio programme 'Desert Island Discs', John Mortimer, barrister and playwright, having stated that he was not a religious person, then read this piece, and commented on the depth of feeling it evoked within him. He was, in fact, describing a religious experience.

Nature, of course, includes the sea, that 'always wind-obeying deep', as Shakespeare described it in 'The Tempest'. Some have looked upon it with gloom, seeing only its treacherous aspect – 'the wavy waste', as Hood expressed it, 'the desert sea' in Biblical imagery. Others have been more sanguine about it, acknowledging its majestic and indomitable nature, as in Homer's 'the loud resounding sea'. Many who encounter it experience the sense of awe and fascination with the memories it invokes of our primeval past, and imagery abounds relating to it as both our origin and our destiny: it is both mysterious and mystical.

There has been no more vivid description of the sea's power to tap a hidden chord than that of Fritjof Capra in the Preface to *The Tao of Physics*:

> I was sitting by the ocean one late summer afternoon, watching the waves rolling in and feeling the rhythm of my breathing, when I suddenly became aware of my whole environment as being engaged in a giant cosmic dance.

He then describes his professional knowledge of atoms, particles and 'cosmic rays' which, till then, had been only theoretical.

As I sat on the beach my former experiences came to life; I 'saw' cascades of energy coming down from outer space, in which particles were created and destroyed in rhythmic pulses; I 'saw' the atoms of the elements and those of my body participating in this cosmic dance of energy; I felt its rhythm and I 'heard' its sound, and at that moment I *knew* that this was the Dance of Shiva, the Lord of Dancers worshipped by Hindus.

And not just Shiva: Capra proceeds to illustrate the parallel paths taken by both Taoism and quantum physics: mysticism indeed. One may relevantly add here that this same sense of universality and timelessness, leading occasionally to what seems like a mystical experience, comes upon some people in other contexts, including *historical* settings. They have described how they have been transported in time when standing quietly in some ancient building or visiting the scene of some crucial event – a battle or a celebration – of long ago. Many have testified to the deep sense of awe and mystery which overtakes them in such places, reminding them that they are merely part of an 'ever-rolling stream' which 'bears all its sons away'. I felt this myself when standing in the pulpit in San Gimignano near Florence from which Savonarola had preached in the fifteenth century against the corruption of both Church and State. It was a mystical experience, when the awareness of time and place became for an indeterminate period non-existent: an experience to which countless others attest, and as truly religious as that found during any act of worship. It was possible to empathise with Savonarola's dying words as the flames consumed him: 'We stand within the very precincts of heaven.' This may be dismissed as no more than an example of an overheated imagination at work, but my recollection is that I experienced in those moments something akin to satori, the void, similar, in fact, to that which happened to me, in totally different circumstances, while watching the reconciliation scene between Cordelia and her father during a performance of 'King Lear'.

The same kind of assessment has been made in other totally different contexts. The study of *mathematics*, for instance, has produced from many of its devotees expressions which, in different contexts, would be unhesitatingly described as religious. Bertrand Russell said of this field, in *The Study of Mathematics*:

> Mathematics possesses not only truth, but supreme beauty – a beauty cold and austere, like that of sculpture.

Not for nothing did Plato inscribe over the entrance to his Academy: 'Let no one ignorant of mathematics enter here.' Philosophers of the subject wrestle with the question of whether numbers, like God in theistic thought, pre-existed the universe. Did two times two make four even in the primordial black hole? Was Pythagorus's theorem true before time began? Or is the

Pythagorean model simply one of many by which we can work – valid, therefore, only so long as it works – as Robert Pirsig suggested in *Zen and the Art of Motorcycle Maintenance* (Pt. III, Ch. 24):

> One geometry cannot be more true than another; it can only be more convenient. Geometry is not true, it is advantageous.

Whatever the answer, there remains a quality about numbers which is nothing less than mystical.

Similar descriptions have been given by explorers in the field of *science*. Granted that the bulk of a scientist's work involves routine and systematic testing, following a line of enquiry, there is a moment before the testing begins when the particular line is established. It is the moment when a new hypothesis is born, but why this line rather than another? Nobody has been able to account for the source of the hypothesis. Max Planck, in his *Scientific Autobiography*, describes the moment as akin to a divine act of creation, a moment of mystery; one could say, of mysticism. Scientists are often accused by those who do not understand them as 'playing God': certainly, in the moments when the intuition, or some other mysterious quality which cannot be analysed, leads them to a possible new discovery, they may be said to be participating in the divine. They are the true miracle-workers in the etymological sense of 'miracle' as 'something to wonder at'. If, as Plato said, 'philosophy begins in wonder' (Thaetetus 155D), then science, a part of philosophy as Plato taught it, remains a partner with it in exploring the unknown. Scientists are, then, quite literally miracle workers. What they discover may by familiarity become indifferent in the eyes of many, as those living amid historical structures, such as today's Romans, become immune to the splendours that surround them. But to those with a philosophical bent, as Santayana stated, 'the familiar excites wonder also'.

This point needs to be emphasised, particularly apropos of nature, because criticism is often made of the romantic apprehension of it: revelling in its beauty and tranquillity, but seemingly being either ignorant of, or turning a blind eye to, the 'groaning and travailing' as St Paul saw it, the fact that, in Tennyson's words, 'nature lends such evil dreams'.

To criticise the romantic view of nature on these grounds – with, presumably, the implication that anyone who approaches nature with this perspective is living in a world of make-believe – seems as unrealistic as it would be to criticise the use of wine in Holy Communion on the grounds that the grapes were once trodden under somebody's feet, or that the vine-tenders were used by the owners as no more than sweated labour. It is as absurd as it would be to look at a naked woman bearing in mind only what St Anselm of Canterbury said about her kind:

> Woman has a clear face and a lovely form, she pleases you not a little,

this milk-white creature! But ah! if her bowels were opened and all the other regions of her flesh, what foul tissues would this white skin be shown to contain.

Odo of Cluny, writing on the same subject, asked: 'Who would wish to embrace *ipsum stercoris saccum* – this stinking bag of manure?'

From one perspective, that is precisely how nature might be described, because death and decay are continuously occurring and the observer will not need to look too keenly or dig too deeply to encounter it. But to allow that consideration to destroy the sense of the spirit of nature is as ludicrous as it would be if a man could not bring himself to make love to his beloved because he could see her only as 'ipsum stercoris saccum'.

It is, then, as a channel for mystical experiences that nature has most captured the hearts and minds of human beings, whether they be poets, New Age enthusiasts, or simply lovers of the countryside. What all have in common is the realisation of the need to be in tune with nature if they are to experience the sense of awe which it can evoke. They may be advocates of the Gaia hypothesis, viewing nature as a single living entity of which *Homo sapiens* is no more than a part, with the consequence that nature is held to be treated with reverence, and not exploited to satisfy human greed. But beyond this philosophical assessment, they are likely to be united in the appreciation of the sense of the numinous which nature conveys. This sense is intensified in many by the awareness of our primordial past: that we spring from this womb which gave us being and nourishes us still. Samuel Coleridge expressed this viewpoint when he wrote:

> In looking at objects of Nature . . . I seem to be seeking, as it were, *asking* for, a symbolic language for something within me that already and forever exists, than observing anything new. Even when that latter is the case, yet still I have always an obscure feeling as if that new phenomenon were the dim awaking of a forgotten or hidden truth of my inner nature.

It is, as Coleridge suggests, within nature's power to remind us of what Pope described as 'things forgot'.

I and thou

We do not have to be involved in any of the foregoing, however, in order to be absorbed in a religious experience. The arts are not pivotal in all people's lives; the majority of Westerners are urban dwellers who, apart from occasional forays into the countryside during vacation periods, have little contact with nature in the raw; most people prefer to spend their free time enjoying sun, sea and sand rather than mooching around ancient edifices; the encounter with mathematics is more often recalled as a nightmare than a dream, as a chore rather than a thrill by people who would be mystified over the suggestion that it be viewed as a potential gateway to enlightenment in anything but the academic sense of that word; and science, a minority subject in most schools, is generally viewed as an esoteric activity, suitable for boffins and other aficionados, but with which it is best (or safest) not to dabble. Surely, it may be argued, the old way of finding religion was much less demanding: attending midnight mass on Christmas Eve, saying the odd prayer, having the baby baptised, committing deceased loved ones to wherever it is that they have gone, turning, when things go wrong, to 'God as we understand him' (to use an Alcoholics Anonymous expression).

Perhaps the way pointed to in this final section will encourage some at least to turn from these simplistic examples of alleged religious experience to one that is real without feeling that they have to undertake a degree course in the process. Martin Buber wrote *Ich und Du* in 1922; it was first translated into' English as *I and Thou* in 1937; but it was only after it appeared in a second enlarged edition in 1958 that it began to make an impact on the English-speaking world. During the 1960s, the period of the 'Honest to God' debate and the Death of God controversy, it invoked a positive response in the minds of many who were inspired by Robinson's advocacy of God as the ground of being, rather than one 'out there', but were unsure what this implied so far as their spiritual lives were concerned. It seemed implausible to worship, or pray to, the ground of being, yet the conviction remained that there was a spiritual dimension which had been tapped in the past, and must continue to be so. Buber's answer struck a chord which proved to be more mellifluous (some might say, more catchy) than anything struck by the others, and as a consequence his viewpoint remains central to any discussion about the future of religion. I have said elsewhere (*East of Existentialism*, p. 138) that I consider Buber, the existentialist Jew, to be a supremely positive link between theism and the non-theism of Eastern thought, and therefore a pioneer in the search for religion without God.

Buber's central theme revolves around the distinction he makes between what he terms 'I–thou' and 'I–it'. In an I–it context, the 'it' is merely part of the back-cloth to the 'I'; there is no sense of commitment or empathy: the I will use the it for his/her own advantage whenever the need arises, so that exploitation is the motivating factor between the two. The I thus finds it useful to have the it around, but feels no sense of obligation as a consequence, and if there is any involvement between the two it is at the shallowest of levels. It reverses Kant's encomium of goodwill as the cement between relationships: the it effectively becomes a thing in the appraisal of the I.

Sociologists have rightly made the natural connection between this analysis and the increasingly impersonal – if not depersonalised – nature of contemporary society, and have offered numerous suggestions (such as

Schumacher's *Small is Beautiful* and Harvey Cox's *The Secular City*) as to how this malaise might be overcome. Buber's own main concern, however, was the implication for religious belief. He argued, as we have seen (p. 40), that everything which the creeds ever declared about God was merely the outcome of human ingenuity, mental constructs to be used as and when required in order to fortify believers in the stance they took. Thus God was no more than an it to the believer's I, a tool which could be discarded when not required; it was a word with a religious connotation but, on close investigation, had nothing whatsoever to do with religion.

In contrast to this is the I–thou relationship. Here, there is a unity, an empathy between the two, an inner harmony which needs no words in order to achieve validity. Each knows the other beyond any need for either explanation or justification, whether the period of harmony be enduring or, as is more likely to be the case, short-lived. He gives the example of two strangers' eyes meeting for a moment in an air-raid shelter as a bomb lands nearby, each knowing without any further communication being needed exactly what the other is thinking. It is in this way, he suggests, that we should see religion: not as an amalgam of concepts but as the ultimate I–thou experience; and just as the two people in the air-raid shelter are united not because their eyes have turned to each other, but because of the menace of which both are totally aware, so it is not the physical act of acknowledging belief in God which is the religious experience, but the awareness of the numinous, an experience which overrides any verbal expressions of belief. This is mysticism, the beyond in the midst. As Ruth Robinson emphasised in *Seventeen Come Sunday* (a commentary on *I and Thou* written for her daughter's birthday – see p. 17):

When you get to the Thou, God is no more.

Buber does more, however, than state mysticism in new terms. He suggests that it is through looking for I–thou relationships with other people that we may find a pathway to the ultimate thou. This is not to say that people should be constantly seeking total empathy with each other, an increasingly popular idea among enthusiasts of what I term exposure therapy, so that in California, it is said, it takes eight people to change a light bulb: one to do the changing and seven to share the experience. Erich Fromm (*The Sane Society*, 1955) warns against the shallow sentimentality to which this attitude is midwife:

Love is union with somebody, or something, outside oneself, under the condition of retaining the separateness and integrity of one's own self.

This is a timely comment in an age in which the sharing of the personal feelings with others, often through the eye of a TV camera, has become the *raison d'être* of swarms of so-called therapeutic, effectively voyeuristic, groups which abound. This is not what Buber implied in his praise of I–thou, since he believed that there was a givenness about such relationships which could not be created simply by self-exposure. In fact, he argued, it was often in silence and a state of mystery, the one with the other, that the mystical may enter into the relationship. D. H. Lawrence describes something along these lines when he speaks of the sense of attachment he feels with his fellow travellers – strangers all – in a railway compartment: loving everything about them, from their creased overcoats to the cut of their hair. But Lawrence was not describing any kind of intimacy of experience: he believed strongly in the privacy of each individual, and he knew no more about the lives of his companions when he left the compartment than when he entered; yet he had sensed how the divine had been manifested, through common humanity. The beyond had been revealed in the midst of the totally familiar.

Tolstoy gives a parallel account in *Anna Karenina*, in a passage which I find to be a profoundly religious description – or a profound description of religion:

> Everything that he saw from the carriage-window, in the pale light of the dying day, appeared to him just as fresh, happy, and strong as himself. The roofs of the houses shining in the setting sun, the sharp outlines of fences and corner buildings, the forms of occasional pedestrians and carriages, the motionless leaves, the green grass, the fields with their straight rows of potatoes, the slanting shadows from the houses, trees, and bushes – everything was beautiful, like an exquisite landscape fresh from the artist's hands.

Here again we find the profane as the medium for the transcendental; the I–thou experience between observer and observed provides a path, as surely as the path followed by Savonarola, to the precincts of heaven; the commonplace becomes a *sanctum santorum*.

The I–thou experience which is common to virtually the entire human race is, of course, that which occurs during intercourse, and we have seen how in Tantrism the Edenic bliss of the experience is held to be the nearest parallel known to human beings to the joy of union between Atman and Brahman. In religious Taoism the union of male and female is viewed as, potentially at least, a complete expression of the harmony of yang and yin, and the perfection of this harmony is believed to increase the chances of participants achieving both health and longevity. I am not proposing to follow up either of these suggestions. The abuses which have crept into some schools of Tantrism illustrate how easily in this context the sublime can become licentious, the divine debauched, so that what begins as a sincere quest for a religious experience can be diverted into the way of lechery and self-indulgence. And the teaching of tao-chiao on sex, with numerous tomes on the subject pouring off Western presses, emphasises the enduring joys of sex, about which the vast bulk of the human race need no confirmation, rather than its spiritual dimension. Tao-chiao uniquely advocates the avoidance of ejaculation on the part of the male in order to be able to continue love-making much longer and so give greater pleasure to the female; this advice seems to be, in the words of Basil Fawlty in the TV series, 'stating the bleedin' obvious'.

This is not to write off sexual union as a religious experience. John Robinson, Bishop of Woolwich, testifying for the defence in the trial of *Lady Chatterley's Lover*, compared the sex described in the book with the Christian sacrament of Holy Communion. Certainly, at its best its transports the participants away from the normal waking state into a Fourth State which may be compared with Shankara's turiya; at its worst it is just as exploitative as any other I–it encounter. Vivekananda, guru of the Hindu Advaita Vedanta school, argued that the spiritual quest could be more single-mindedly pursued through a life without sex than through one in which it plays a continual part, and most religious communities require celibacy, certainly for their monks and nuns, sometimes for their representatives who work in the community. Vivekananda's claim misses the point, however: it is not a case of whether celibacy or sexual activity the more readily facilitates the experience of the beyond in the midst: it is whether the experience of sex leading to orgasm is an actual example of this mystery. Havelock Ellis in *The Dance of Life* affirmed:

> Sexual pleasure, wisely used and not abused, may prove the stimulus and liberator of our finest and most exalted activities.

And religion is the most exalted of all.

Chapter 10

Beyond good and evil

> When the great Tao is forgotten, goodness and piety appear.
> *(Tao Te Ching, 18)*

Among the most vacuous of statements is the affirmation 'God is good'. Every word in this dictum which, apparently without embarrassment, people stick in their cars or on church noticeboards, demands analysis which even at the most elementary level indicates that the concept is not just ambiguous but meaningless.

We have examined the problems associated with the concept of God, so it can be seen why the vagueness inherent in the term gives the statement a bad start. 'Is' seems a straightforward word, until one begins to study ontology or linguistic analysis after the fashion of Heidegger, when the awesome complexities of the word begin to emerge. In the present context, for example, it can be interpreted variously (though by no means exclusively) as:

- 'represents' (as in the non-transubstantial view of the elements in Holy Communion: 'this is my body . . .');
- 'means the same thing as' or 'is nothing else than', as in the transubstantial view;
- 'has as his (its) nature';
- 'stands in the place of'.

The word 'good' is equally ambiguous. Fundamentally, as we see when it is used in a non-ethical context, it means no more than fulfilling the requirements of that with which it is associated, like a good cricket bat, a good knife, or a good book: whatever one seeks in those objects in general is to be found in this specimen in particular. Even when applied to human beings, the word often has an amoral connotation, so that I can say, ironically, perhaps, but not untruthfully, that someone is a good burglar, someone else a good killer. So if I were to describe someone as 'a good person', I am saying no more than that this person has more than the average share of the qualities which I admire most in people. Others may well disagree with this judgment, not because they see the person differently but because their hierarchy of desirable human qualities is different. In itself, therefore, the word 'good' is meaningless because it has no content, and will remain empty until agreement can be reached on the nature of the qualities to be exhibited by the object or person under discussion. With reference to God, the description of him as good means no more than that he possesses to the uttermost degree the qualities viewed by human beings as most desirable in their species; and since agreement on this matter is about as likely as on the comparative merits of painters, poets or musicians, the image of a good God will remain, as it has always been, equivocal if not amphibolous.

In practice, few of those who believe in a personal God are likely to acknowledge the relevance of this consideration, on the grounds that, whether we can define it or not, everybody recognises goodness when it confronts him; while those who don't believe argue that 'God' is simply a personification of 'the good', so that the statement is merely tautologous. The fact is, however, that the glibness with which the word's use is characterised has led, and is still leading, people, usually encouraged by their spiritual leaders, to slide effortlessly down the slope that identifies moral behaviour with the will of God, and in so doing has for centuries held up the cause of moral maturity.

This state of affairs might be left simply as a fact to bemoan and discuss in another book on, say, moral education, rather than one to be discussed here, were it not for one crucial feature of the situation which, if it were to remain unrefuted, would undermine the concept of religion as I have outlined it. This is the contention, taught by millions over the centuries, accepted by billions, and still expressed today by adherents of the theistic religions, that the only safeguard of morality is God, whose essence is goodness, whose will and purpose for his creatures have been made known, and to whom all people will ultimately be answerable. Without this divine sanction for morality, it is argued, the urge to 'be good' will evaporate, the concept of goodness will vanish, and the human race will become nothing more than a vast amalgum of self-seeking individuals doing their own thing. C. S. Lewis in *Mere Christianity* expressed this concern in colourful words:

> We only learn to behave ourselves in the presence of God, and if the sense of that presence is removed, mankind tends to lark about.

This nightmare scenario is of course a basic motif among those sects which treat their scriptures like a police constable's handbook. Some of those who are looking for a new way of understanding religion write off this attitude to the scriptures as nothing more than the dying twitches of a lost cause, but this is an example of wishful thinking. It is among sects of the fundamentalist persuasion that attendances are most on the increase. As we have already seen, they are often led by a charismatic male person who is generally not averse to blatantly exploiting his power among those who lack it, for reasons which it would be invidious to explore here. If my description of religion is sound, any kind of devotion which centres on a *person* is, in any case, illegitimate, whether that person be the local curate, the visiting evangelist, Buddha, or Jesus Christ. Such a person may – though, from a study of history, it is extremely unlikely – be a channel of religion, as a painting or a natural scene may be channels: but the religious experience is beyond all tangible phenomena, and this is especially the case with human channels, where the phenomena almost invariably blanket out the noumena.

We have seen that even Immanuel Kant fell back on the concept of God to justify his categorical imperative. How can anyone be sure, he was asked, that a particular interpretation of the ideal society was the right one as opposed to a self-serving distortion? Granted that he is personally sure about his interpretation of 'the moral law within', how can he validly respond to another who sees and interprets it differently? Kant's reply was that the moral law was at the same time both the creation of God, the essence of morality, and a proof (the only proof which Kant accepted) of his existence. But the doubter's question remains open: where interpretations of God's moral purpose differ, who is to arbitrate? Blake laconically expressed this conundrum in a famous couplet (in 'The Everlasting Gospel'):

> Both read the Bible day and night,
> But you read black where I read white.

Even Don Cupitt sees a continuing need, however temporary, for the use of God in the field of human behaviour. He states:

> I have used the phrase the Eye of God for a nonrealistic continuation of the ancient habit of looking at our selves and our own lives as if with a God's-eye view. The old way of living *coram Deo* (as if before the face of God) was valuably consciousness-raising and morally stabilizing, and one may usefully continue to pray to God just as one may find oneself talking to and thinking of a dead person.
>
> (*After God*, p. 125)

This is akin to Confucius's employment of 'the way of heaven' (p. 13), parallel to my boyhood response to an elderly aunt who spotted me sweeping the dirt under her carpet. To my excuse that 'nobody can see it', she replied, 'God can see it.' Cupitt's approach means accepting a situation where, even though the cat has died, nobody should tell the mice. My approach rests on the conviction that – to continue the metaphor – since the cat has died we must find other ways of dealing with the mice.

My aim in this chapter is primarily, as its title suggests, to indicate how, in the most advanced expressions of religion, the whole concept of good and evil, or good versus evil, must be outgrown on the grounds that it reflects a condition of moral and spiritual immaturity. Before that, and even though the arguments have been well rehearsed since at least the time of Hume, I wish to lay to rest the belief that there is any real connection, other than where 'God' is used as an imaginary inspirational companion (like the invisible 'friend' with whom my five-year-old granddaughter Ami discusses private and personal matters) between the will of God as believers in him understand it and the individual's sense of moral obligation. Does 'I ought' mean the same as 'God wills'?

We have to distinguish straightaway between two different expressions of the connection between the moral sense and God's will. If we say, on the one hand, that God wills so-and-so (let us say, fidelity to one's sexual partner) because this arrangement is right (let us say, for the maintenance of a life-long relationship), then manifestly God is not essential to the process, but rather is acting in the role of the all-wise one who can identify the right course of behaviour from amid the variety of courses on offer. The 'right' course, however, is and remains, right, according to the original supposition, independently of God's assessment of it. He is the expert whose advice, if we are wise, we will follow. But since this approach does not exclude the possibility that people may find the answer for themselves, he is not essential, however helpful his advice may be. So on this interpretation of the terms involved, there is no necessary link between human behaviour and God's will: 'right' and 'wrong' are independent of any divine assessment of their worth.

The more usual expression of the link between the sense of moral obligation and divine commands is expressed differently: a particular form of behaviour is right (or wrong) because God so wills it. It is in this way that apologists such as Kant and Lewis, along with millions of others, however less felicitously, have interpreted the connection, and, if it were viable, would certainly confirm that morality cannot stand without God to maintain it.

The objections to this interpretation are, however, overwhelming, as Richard Holloway (op. cit.) has confirmed. It makes morality – right and wrong – a totally arbitrary matter. Fidelity in marriage is right because it is God's will, he has chosen that way of conducting a sexual relationship. But since he is God, with nobody and nothing outside him to influence any decision he may make on moral matters, he could just as well have chosen infidelity as the surest seal on these relationships. Why not? Who is to prevent him? We may in fact challenge certain expressions of his will as being unworthy of the highest aspirations of which human beings are capable (such as the condemnation of unbelievers into 'outer darkness' which New Testament writers continually indulge in): but this would be as effective as a slave's trying to persuade Nero to lay aside his fiddle and call the fire brigade.

Many of the conclusions about God's moral rules reached by those who accept him as their author, in fact suggest, as I shall illustrate presently, that either he is, or they are, in a state of confusion on the matter. J. S. Mill seems to have felt the same when he wrote:

> I will call no being good, who is not what I mean when I apply that epithet to my fellow-creatures; and if such a being can sentence me to hell for not so calling him, to hell I will go.
>
> (*Examination of Sir William Hamilton's Philosophy*, ch. 7)

This interpretation of God's overriding authority on moral matters writes off all human autonomy – the process of establishing, through reflection and experience, the right behaviour in a particular situation. The person who says 'I'm a catholic, *and therefore* (note the italics) opposed to abortion' or 'I'm a socialist *and therefore* believe in wholesale nationalisation' has lost any claim to autonomy *and therefore* to authenticity because he/she has become no more than the mouthpiece for an external authority. Similarly, the believer in God who says 'thy will, not mine be done' is thereby laying aside his most precious possession: the ability to assess moral dilemmas for himself, and the authority to act accordingly. To be autonomous in this way is to have the courage to lay aside the illusion that 'if God be for us, (nobody) can be against us', as St Paul expressed it or, in the words of John Knox, that 'one man plus God is a majority'.

Even more damning of this perspective is its implications for (and, in the past, the consequent treatment of) atheists and other non-believers. If morality is defined as what God wills, the logical inference is that any person who refuses to believe in God cannot be moral. The fact that we are surrounded by such people, that is, non-believers, who yet live in a way that others describe as moral (though I shall be suggesting that, alongside the word 'good', this word is basically empty) means that we either discard this argument altogether or fall back on the apologia to which I was introduced in theological college. This is the 'spiritual capital' argument: the view that some atheists do, indeed, express moral conduct in their lives but only because they were raised in a generation surrounded by religious teaching, or God-talk. Give it another generation, so the argument goes, and we shall see a watering-down of morality as the rock on which it is built is chipped away.

This point of view begs so many questions that it is difficult to plough one's way through the morass. Chief of them is the bland assumption that things were, in fact, morally healthier when religious values controlled moral values. Any disinterested study of history – say, Victorian England with its acclaimed values – will indicate that the person who believes this has either been reading fairy tales or is wearing special blinkers provided by the neighbourhood parson. The only values the Victorians understood were monetary, and their so-called religious values a kind of spiritual form of it: booking a place in heaven. In the present context, 'Victorian values' is an oxymoron. Even the missionary enterprise which one associates with the period was based on the same conviction: only goodness expressed as obedience to the will of God was true goodness. Consequently people raised in either godless cultures or – worse – cultures which encouraged the worship of the wrong God, must be brought to see the light, lest they be condemned to spend eternity in hell. The megalomanic assumption underlying this enterprise would beggar belief if it were not still to be found in even the most exalted circles. The Durham University Union's Debating Society, for instance, in 1999, carried by an overwhelming majority (despite my arguments to the contrary, in fact) the motion, 'This house believes that Jesus Christ is the way, the truth, and the life.' Speaker after speaker made it quite clear that, in his or her view, members of other religions, or those with no religion, were doomed eternally: it is, after all, in the book.

Reference to 'the book' leads to one further, overwhelming, refutal of the view that 'good' moral behaviour means obeying the will of God. The natural question to which this leads is: how can one be sure exactly what it is that God actually wills? After all, since the assumption is that human destinies depend on obedience to his commands, it seems no trivial matter that the nature and content of these commands be unambiguous. For theists, there have been three channels by which God's will has been revealed to those seeking to obey it: through their consciences, their elders in council and their scriptures.

If the conscience is taken as a guide, it emerges that people are to him 'as flies to wanton boys', since he offers opposing advice on any issue to different people. One person could conscientiously kill in God's name (or at his command, as this injunction might be interpreted), another would feel compelled to be a conscientious objector to military service on the grounds that his conscience forbids him to take up arms against a fellow human being.

If it is through the councils of the elders of the religious communities that God's will becomes known, the same irrationality occurs. It was, for example, only at the Council of Trent in 1564 that the Christian bishops decided (by a majority of three) that women had souls. Today, we have the anomolous position where one hierarchy of church leaders can blandly declare the use of condoms to be a sin, while another, representing a different branch, declares it to be a sin not to use them.

It is, however, to the written word – the Qur'an, the Old and New Testaments – to which most people turn who are seeking the ultimate revelation of God's will and purpose. Thus, as already mentioned (p. 42), homosexuality is condemned (and homosexuals persecuted) because, according to Leviticus 18: 22, it is 'an abomination': a statement quoted with approval by a Baroness in the British Upper House late in the year 2000 (CE, it should be noted, not BCE as one could be forgiven for imagining) as grounds not to discuss homosexuality in sex lessons in state schools. Presumably, on the same authority one's daughter can be sold into slavery, as sanctioned by Exodus 21: 7; people who work on the Sabbath should be executed, as instructed by God in Exodus 35: 2; and anyone who blasphemes be stoned to death by the whole congregation, as God instructed his people in Leviticus 24: 16. Looking beyond the Old Testament, wives who are recalcitrant should be beaten by their husbands, as sanctioned in the Qur'an 438; and those who do not follow the path of the 'true' believer can be treated as non-persons, 'the dogs and sorcerers and fornicators and murderers and idolators, and everyone who loves and practises falsehood', as countenanced in the New Testament (Revelation 22: 15); and we can share in the vituperation of Jesus who, according to Matthew 23: 33, denounced the Jewish scholars (the scribes and Pharisees) as 'You serpents, you brood of vipers, how are you to escape being sentenced to hell?'

Clearly, modern devotees of these scriptures will put some kind of gloss on such passages, comparing them with alternative, more acceptable sayings. This is fair enough: but by that process they are effectively laying aside the concept that what is good is what God commands (in the books which he has sanctified) and, employing their own powers of judgment, are expressing their individual autonomy. In whatever terms God's will may be expressed, he has become superfluous to requirements.

Moral maturity

All that I've said so far about morals in relation to God is, of course, repetitive of conclusions reached not only by agnostic philosophers, but also by people who continue to believe devoutly in God. They will be unmoved – perhaps even bored – by these oft-rehearsed arguments (though they must still have to live with the maledictions of their fundamentalist counterparts). What I now wish to explore is whether the words 'good' and 'evil' have any meaning that is likely to help anyone trying to decide how to behave in a situation which offers more than one course of action. I have suggested that 'good' means 'meets requirements', so that the real debate revolves around the nature of the requirements rather than the meaning of 'good'. May we not therefore say that 'bad' or, as expressed more intensely, 'evil', means that, in the object or person under review, those requirements are either in short supply or are missing entirely? This discussion will take us into the minefield of post-modernism, but it is terrain which cannot be avoided if we are to work our way through to what I am terming, even though this is a value judgment on my part, moral maturity.

This phrase immediately lays itself open to question because of the uncertainties surrounding its meaning – uncertainties which are so far-reaching that it is quite feasible for two teachers to pay lip service to it as the supreme goal of education, yet have totally different ideas about what should be looked for in any pupil who has achieved it. For one it could mean a condition where society's rules have been learned, understood and taken to heart; for the other, a state of mind which challenges the rules until they either prove their worth or are found wanting and therefore in need of revision. To remove this ambiguity I shall align myself with classical Hindu rishis and Taoist masters, endorsed some millennia later by Nietzsche, by describing moral maturity as the state *beyond good and evil*.

The first stage in the process of reaching this state is the realisation of the futility of arguing how things *ought* to be and to accept the human condition as simply a reflection of how things are. Moralisers perpetually claim that most people's behaviour is not good enough, by which they generally mean that most people do not express the same standards or values as themselves. Their views therefore express a value judgment which, like all value judgments, reflects a discrete system of moral priorities built up over the years according to the path followed, the influences and ideas which have occurred, and the image of the world and its inhabitants which has been created in the process. Heraclitus was right to suggest that nobody can step twice into the same river, but more important is the phenomenological fact that no two people step into the same river once. *Every human being lives in a different universe from everyone else*; so we should not be either surprised or dismayed that 'right' and 'wrong', 'good' and 'bad' have different connotations for different people. While on many issues there is of course an overlap (because the paths which people travel have certain common features), the situation remains that, apropos of the major non-verifiable areas – art, religion, politics, besides morals – what seems to one as plain as a pikestaff is to the other shrouded in obscurity. This leads to a consequence of great significance in the field of morals: if one man's meat is another's *poisson*, one person's good may well be another's evil. Of course, on many moral issues the majority of the human race commonly express agreement about what is desirable conduct and what is not; but it does not follow that they are 'right' in their judgment, for the simple reason that rightness in this situation is a purely subjective matter, not dependent on a majority vote. (If that were not the case, a number of crude and inhumane laws would rapidly find their way on to many nations' statute books, as opinion polls on – for instance – the treatment of criminals constantly reveal.)

This issue is, however, secondary to the point that exponents of the state beyond good and evil had in mind. Instead of holding the two conditions to be mutually antagonistic, proponents characterise them as mutually symbiotic, each depending on the other for its viability, in the strict sense that without the other, neither could survive in any meaningful form. Just as we could not know the meaning of 'hot' or 'wet' except in contrast with 'cold' or 'dry', of 'dark' except in contrast with 'light', of 'life' with 'death', so the meaning of 'good' emerges only in contrast with 'evil'. 'Goodness' on its own is meaningless; only in contrast with its opposite can it be validly discussed. This is an example of the twin forces of yin and yang which, both in partnership with, and in contradistinction to, each other, keep the universe on course.

This leads to a further consideration which is likely to be unwelcome to moralisers. Not only are yin and yang, though polar opposites, dependent upon each other: it is impossible to say that either is 'better', more important, or more worth pursuing than the other. Many people may prefer summer (yang) to winter (yin), or gentleness (yin) to assertiveness (yang): but both have an essential part in the scheme of things so that without the one, we should also lack the other. This bold idea was expressed profoundly by Walt Whitman in his poem 'All is Truth'. It ends with these lines:

> Meditating among liars, and retreating sternly into myself,
> I see that there are no liars or lies after all,
> And nothing fails its perfect return – And that what are called lies are
>   perfect returns,
> And that each thing exactly represents itself, and what has preceded it,
> And that the truth includes all, and is compact, just as much as space
>   is compact,
> And that there is no law or vacuum in the amount of the truth – but
>   that all is truth without exception;
> And henceforth I will go celebrate anything I see or am,
> And sing and laugh, and deny nothing.

This is the yin-yang philosophy and it has the crucial implication for moral decision-making that there is no such thing as absolute good or absolute evil; indeed, it would be hard to imagine how such qualities would express themselves in any person's behaviour, since the absoluteness of the goodness or the evil would require a universal acceptance of the content of the two conditions. Since, as I suggested earlier, every individual is a universe unto himself alone, it is inconceivable that all would agree that certain forms of behaviour are always desirable in every situation – which is what is implied by the concept of absolute goodness.

If there were such a thing as objective goodness or evil, there would be no more debate about its content than there is about the content of air or water. Those who view God as the source of our knowledge of right and wrong – whether from the Roman Catholic or Biblical fundamentalist perspectives – cheerfully make their absolutist affirmations based on his alleged divine authority, and, because they often shout these affirmations loudly and are still held by some to reflect this authority, are listened to by no small number. But it remains the case that it is simply not true that adultery, or fraud, or robbery with violence *are* wrong, or that self-sacrifice, or giving to the poor, or helping the distressed *are* right. It is the case that many people hold these views and would do everything possible to make their content effective; but they are still making judgments from within the citadel of their own consciousness, established over their lives' experiences. This means that there is no such person as an unbiased or disinterested individual – one who could see 'like God' as he is imagined. Chuang-Tzu, in a famous passage, asked where a truly neutral person could be found to arbitrate between two people who had a grievance with each other:

> Whom shall we ask to arbitrate? If we ask someone who agrees with you, since he has already agreed with you, how can he arbitrate? If we ask someone who agrees with me, since he already agrees with me, how can he arbitrate? . . . Thus among you, me, and others, none knows which is right.

Chuang Tzu could have been commenting on the US Presidential election of the year 2000, and his warning should therefore surprise nobody. However, his reaction to its infamous outcome would not have been to cry 'foul', which he would have described as 'flaying the air', but to have accepted that, in the richest country in the world, it was unsurprising that government should emanate from the most powerful financial organisations. That, Chuang-Tzu would have said, is how things are; meanwhile he would go fishing, awaiting the moment when, as yin moves inexorably into yang, the tide turns. This is wu wei.

Only the concept of God sustains that of good in its moral sense, and with the demise of the one, the other cannot be long in following. People will either learn to live naturally and intuitively, which for most will mean learning to live harmoniously together: or they will continue, as they have over the millennia, to exploit each other, with disastrous consequences on all sides. And the religious experience, a state truly beyond good and evil, will be a bonus enjoyed independently of morality. With the death of God goes the death of the godfather.

What shall we tell the children?

There may well be a number of readers who are happy to accept the relativist approach to morals as described, but are uncertain what the implications may be for those who have not yet reached that stage of development which I am designating as *mature*. By that evaluative word I mean the ability, when making moral decisions, to reflect on the facts of a situation, to identify the realistic options, to recognise who is likely to be affected by whatever choice is made, and to accept personal responsibility for the consequences of the choice, even though, in Sartre's phrase, it is accompanied by anguish (from knowing that there can be no buck-passing), a sense of abandonment (by God, who is no more) and despair (from the realisation that one is only as strong as one's own will). However, it is axiomatic that this state characterises only those of older years, experience and judgment, and the question of how children and younger people may be gradually encouraged to achieve that state is of central importance, both in the educational world and beyond.

It may help if we bear in mind the findings of the American educational psychologist, Laurence Kohlberg. His analysis, based on wide-ranging research, led him to conclude that there are three stages of moral development, from views of right and wrong based on sanctions, to the assessment of actions in terms of moral standards. He identified three levels of development: the first is what he termed *premoral*, where actions are orientated towards punishment and obedience, with happiness as an end; the second is *morality of conventional role and conformity to it* – maintaining good relations and the approval of others (the peer group mentality), with authority the ultimate sanction and support; and finally, *the morality of self-accepted principles*, involving the idea of contract and individual rights, directed by personal principles of conscience. Kohlberg suggested that, normally, having moved from one level to the next, children did not regress (being incarcerated in, for instance, a concentration camp, or suffering brain damage were exceptional events, not relevant to his main thesis). It follows, of course, that any adult who has not moved to the highest moral level must be judged to be morally immature.

Since society does not lack such citizens, as it is similarly not lacking in the innumerate or tone deaf, it becomes imperative that the educational process be positively directed towards producing the morally mature. What this means in terms of a moral education syllabus over the school years has been discussed comprehensively elsewhere (see, especially, Wilson, Williams and Sugarman, *Introduction to Moral Education*, Penguin, 1967). The debate has in the main concerned itself with three issues: the relation between religion and morals, the analysis of the sense of obligation, and appropriate methods for promoting certain moral values, generally those of liberal humanism. The issue which remains largely unresolved, however, is whether progress from moral immaturity to moral maturity be viewed as a natural process or one that schools can foster. Is it feasible to speak of training children morally, as we train them in literacy or numeracy? Having decided that there is no logical connection between religious belief and moral convictions, what should be the policy for education in this field?

The fact is that the basis for morality, as a necessary means for the survival of society, is in no way diminished by the exposure of the limitations or illusions of supernatural sanctions. Society persists because it is in the interests of most individuals that it should continue to do so. Ultimately, whether we like it or not, the sanction for morality is that society must and will use violence against those whose conduct threatens it – and this unwelcome fact remains the case despite my earlier statement that society is and will always be imperfect simply because that is how things are. It is therefore wholly unnecessary to teach children to feel guilty about stealing when they know that, if they persist in stealing, they will stand a good chance of being placed in prison. (This is not to suggest that fear of punishment is a sign of maturity in moral behaviour: quite the reverse, as Kohlberg indicates; but it would be unrealistic to deny that it operates in the minds of many for whom the eleventh and chief commandment is, Thou shalt not be found out.)

The question, then, is not whether moral standards have in practice declined, but whether moral maturity is increasing, and whether schools can assist in the process. According to moralisers over the centuries, standards have always been in decline, as this comment illustrates:

> It is a general complaint that this nation of late years is grown more numerously and excessively vicious than heretofor; pride, luxury, drunkenness, whoredom, cursing, swearing, bold and open atheism everywhere abounding.
>
> (Baroness Young in the House of Lords, 2001,
> cf. John Milton in 1671)

A *Punch* cartoon fifty years ago illustrated this succinctly with one man saying to his companion, 'Things are not what they were'. 'No,' replied the other, 'they never were.'

The problem of achieving moral maturity has been intensified by two new complications. First, life in the metropolis makes it necessary for society to impose ever greater restrictions on individual freedom, and the greater the number of restrictions, the harder it is to enforce them all. Second, the world has become technologically one unit. It seems that the nation-states themselves must surrender their freedom in the interests of the survival of humanity, and the machinery for imposing this, despite the existence of the United Nations Organisation, has not yet been devised. More than ever, therefore, moral education seems to be required among young people.

Tasks for moral education

The first and most urgent task, illustrated by the entire argument of this book, is the negative one of *destroying vestiges of superstitious views of morality*. The biggest obstacle to progress is not moral weakness or wickedness, but the ignorance which enslaves people to concepts of 'right' or 'wrong' which are little more than taboos. These concepts are not only false but harmful. The taboos are exemplified in the objections by members of religious organisations (often – falsely, if the argument of this book is sound – described as 'religious objections') to birth control, abortion, euthanasia and homosexuality. Children properly instructed in the rational social basis of morality need never fall into such errors.

The second task is *to make pupils aware of the existing consensus on morality*. The fact is that while there are of course controversial issues, on a wide range of forms of behaviour human beings of all nations and races are virtually unanimous. We are all (or almost all) against war, murder, theft from individuals, cruelty – especially to children and animals – social inequality, racial intolerance, religious bigotry and authoritarianism. We are all (or almost all) in favour of compassion, kindness, liberation for oppressed minorities, conservation and protection of the environment, individual and, in particular, sexual freedom. Readers of popular newspapers in many countries throughout the world may argue that the stories presented don't encourage this optimism, but here it is necessary to become sophisticated enough to know that it is news of human follies and vices which sells newspapers, not reports on virtuous behaviour. The teacher can counteract the distortions of the press by informing more comprehensively and fairly both as to what the prevailing values are and as to the sanctions imposed on those who violate them.

The third, and perhaps most difficult task, is *to extrapolate from present values and try to forecast those which will emerge* in the world in which the pupils will soon be playing an active part. If the teacher plays the prophet, she/he risks being wrong, of course: but the tension between conformity to present society and preparation for a new society is endemic to education. If it is the case that 'every idea is an incitement', then education must be a revolutionary process or it is nothing. The need to create effective world institutions, the overthrow of systems based on the economic power of an exploiting class, and the creation of a genuine (as opposed to a hypocritical) permissive society are obvious candidates for future developments.

Finally, the teacher may try to educate pupils *to make responsible choices between the mores of different sub-groups*. The adolescent seeking identity is confronted by the pressures of a commercialised consumer society and of the idiot herd as well as the opportunities for working towards constructive change. The teacher cannot choose for the pupil, but she can give him the information which will enable him to choose for himself as rival claims are made, some more raucously than others, from this tower of Babel.

Beyond good and evil: the religious dimension

The steps taken so far in this discussion have focused mainly on the way morality has been liberated from a law-giving God. In the West it has taken longer to realise this than in the East, since the East's main religions – Hinduism, Buddhism, Taoism, Zen and (if it may be included) Confucianism – pay little or no regard to the concept of an omnipotent lawgiver. Rules of behaviour are posited more as advice to the unwary than as moral commands from on high. Most significant is the Taoist view of behaviour as the natural action in the right place, depending on whether the yin or the yang is in the ascendant. Thus it is impossible to state categorically whether aggression is right or wrong. In some circumstances it is natural, in others it is not. On a games field, for example, or in time of war, or when facing a homicidal maniac, aggression would be in place; in a primary school classroom, or in a council chamber, or a hospital ward, it would be out of place. In itself it is a neutral concept, beyond good and evil.

Can this concept achieve a religious connotation? Many Hindu teachers have believed so, and we may now look more closely at their thinking on the matter. As in all ethical systems, Hinduism identifies sources of norms for human behaviour: tradition (needed for social stability) and interdependence (needed for social cohesion). The sanctions are consequences, not guilt or retribution. However, those who try for liberation (moksha, enlightenment) outgrow these norms. Instead of seeking to live according to a received pattern, they practise bodily, mental and emotional self-control, with the aim of achieving personal harmony and peace. All can achieve this aim by stabilising the 'lower' aspects of the person – body, mind, personality – and reaching the ground of being, which is reality, consciousness, happiness (*sat chit ananda* – see p. 65). Cupitt (op. cit., p. 179) prefers the Buddhist term sunyata, *the blissful Void*, which he interprets as *the disappearance of the self into immanence, objectivity and nothingness*.

Whichever phrase or description we use, the state means leaving behind the pairs of opposites which confront us in our usual awakened state – hatred and love, misery and pleasure – since to be one with the ground of being means losing one's personal ego, which is the source of all dualities. In its place is absorption into that which is impersonal and one in all individuals (which may be akin to Jung's concept of the collective unconscious).

Thus liberated, a person is bound by no rules or duties, but acts spontaneously from joy and for the welfare of others. This can lead to political action (Gandhi, for example), to teaching (Ramakrishna), to celebration in music and poetry (Nanak, Tagore), to work for the poor (Vivekananda) or the mentally ill (Meher Baba). In a phrase, liberation is awareness of *non-dual reality* (like the water-drop entering the sea) and is incompatible with assertion of personality, or injury to, or exploitation of others. This is the state beyond good and evil, and its significant feature is not that it leads to a disregard of other sentient beings, but that benevolent acts are viewed as an intuitive expression of the experience of oneness with all beings, rather than as a painstaking observance of rules based either on rational arguments or authoritative commands.

One important concession must be made. This is not a state for the unenlightened, otherwise it is easy to understand that abuses would creep in. The unenlightened, like those, described earlier, at the lower levels of moral maturity, will find it beneficial to observe norms of behaviour. If, like Meister Eckhart quoted on p. 50, those norms are to be laid aside, this must happen only with the authority which springs from knowing why other considerations take precedence; those who act anarchically without such knowledge are likely to be little more than immature trouble-makers, rebelling, like

adolescents, for rebellion's sake. St Augustine in his Seventh homily sum-
marised morality in the dictum: *Love God, and do what you like*. In the light
of the direction taken in this book, we may reinterpret that dictum as *Follow
your intuitive nature, which you will discover in the ground of being*.
However, the state beyond good and evil finds itself on different ground from
that held by Augustine, since, as his writings elsewhere indicate, he was still
tied to the belief that one must make up one's mind between good and evil.
The state which I am describing is beyond the level of needing to debate the
rights and wrongs of any moral matter in the first place, since it is realised
that such a debate assumes the existence of objective values, which do not
exist (in fact, never did exist except in people's imaginations).

Don Cupitt considers this post-modernist approach to be unbearable for
many people. He writes (*After God*, pp. 88–9):

> In postmodern culture, after the end of the old metaphysics, nothing any
> longer has any assured and objective value, basis, or foundation. There
> is no fixed order of things out there. Everything is contingent . . . To
> repeat popular phrases . . . *This is it; this is all there is* – and now we are
> suddenly overcome with vertigo, because we have no idea whether to say
> that this fleeting life of ours has become infinitely important or infinitely
> *un*important.

I hope to be able to show in the final chapter that the situation is not quite
so unbearable, that it is at least an honest attempt to come to terms with the
actual situation rather than the artificial situation of a game, where the rules
are made up in order to make it playable, and how, speaking for myself, life
remains infinitely more important than it could have ever been under the old
regime. Cupitt ends *After God* with the warning:

> Unless something new is launched quickly, I fear that the process of
> postmodernization will have gone so far, and will have become so
> destructive, that it will be too late.

(p. 128)

I believe, on the contrary, that post-modernism reflects things as they are,
and that the 'new way' must seize the opportunity which it offers. I doubt,
however, if this is a 'launching', since others are already on the high seas, if
not walking the waters.

Chapter 11

Substance without form

We are too late for the gods
and too early for Being. Being's poem,
just begun, is man.

(Martin Heidegger, *Poetry, Language, Thought*, p. 4)

If the path that we have been treading has been in the right direction, we have reached certain conclusions which, in part, accord with travellers along a parallel path, but in part reflect the unavoidable fact that, since no two people can walk the same road, the destination of every trekker is uniquely his or hers. However, maybe a suggestion here and there will enable others not to waste time grappling towards a dead end in the labyrinth.

The basic affirmation on which all else rests is that metaphysics is real; and religion, an expression of the metaphysical, is therefore also real. It is an experience which is part – maybe the main part – of the human birthright, providing an extra dimension to human experience. The problem with this apparently unambiguous statement, however, lies in the key word: religion. In the minds of the vast majority of the human race, it is confined to a particular set of beliefs, an exclusive set of values, and a life-style dominated by restrictive moral rules. It is associated with words like holiness, saintliness, divinity, salvation, or faith, and many people feel not only uninterested in such qualities, but positively alien to them. For instance, when discussing the title of this book with friends, colleagues, students and other fellow-travellers, the near-universal advice has been to 'keep religion out of it'. But since the whole aim of the book is to suggest that the received image is false, it would, I think, have been pusillanimous of me to have disguised my intention by shunning the word. If that makes the mountain harder to climb, so be it.

Let me recapitulate which forms of religion (and I am thinking primarily of its theistic representations), normally associated with the word, need to be abandoned, on the grounds that they obscure, if not entirely eclipse, its real meaning, and are therefore lumber to be discarded.

The first piece of lumber, as has been reiterated continually throughout this book, is *God*. Every time his name is invoked, and every dogma associated with him, is nothing more than a human construct, created to satisfy some human need as outlined in Chapter 4. At its best, the God-image has certainly inspired people to great acts of valour and self-giving: and has, as Cupitt suggests (quoted on p. 111), provided a constant incentive to aim high. But the image has traditionally, and almost universally, been backed by the belief that God really exists, not just as an imaginary ideal, but in actuality as a kind of super-person, and so long as the image is retained, that belief must inevitably endure. It must therefore be stated unambiguously that because there is no divine super-being (God is dead), the image is no longer helpful unless we resolve to spend our time in a world of make-believe. God was a myth by which people could cheerfully live in the past, as, centuries ago, people lived and successfully navigated the globe with the Ptolemaic myth that the earth was the centre of the solar system. The fact that that myth worked does not mean that navigators today still adhere to it; and the same must follow with regard to God: it is a myth by which we can no longer live.

At its worst, belief in God produces a narrowness and divisiveness of spirit which is harmful to human co-operation. These words by H. L. Mencken (1880–1956) may seem harsh, but there are millions who answer his description, and their numbers – as opposed to those commended earlier – are growing alarmingly:

> God is the immemorial refuge of the incompetent, the helpless, the miserable. They find not only sanctuary in His arms, but also a kind of superiority, soothing to their macerated egos. He will set them above their betters.
>
> (Mencken, 'Minority Report', *Notebook*)

Not all believers in God have fallen into this trap, but the strength and power of, for example, the religious right in the USA indicates the continuing menacing potency of the 'balm for macerated egos'.

The concept of God as the unknowable source of all things, expressed in the term the Godhead, is of course another matter; but for obvious reasons that term is confusing, and the same people who are deterred from accepting religion as a natural experience in their lives because of its association with 'God' are likely to feel the same about 'Godhead'. The idea is basic, and I shall return to it later; for the present it is sufficient to say that the name-tag simply confuses the issue.

Associated with belief in God as integral to religion is the *acceptance of certain historical or quasi-historical figures as religious icons*. In Judaism these include Moses and the prophets, in Islam, Muhammed, in Mahayana Buddhism 'the Lord Buddha', in Hinduism (though not so strongly) the rishis or seers and in Christianity Jesus, uniquely acclaimed as the Son of God. Millions have modelled their lives on these figures, and have viewed this process (and been so viewed by others) as engaging themselves in religious activity. There is, however, nothing religious about this at all. To model one's life on an admired figure may be a laudable way of living (though much depends on the particular features which are imitated) but this is a totally human characteristic, associated with religion only because the icons have normally been either the founders or noteworthy representatives of a particular organised religion. There is no essential difference between modelling one's life on one of these figures and modelling it on some other inspirational figure such as Karl Marx, Carl Gustav Jung, or Charles Darwin: the only difference is that, while the first group presented new insights into religion, the second group revolutionised our understanding of society, the mind and the natural world. To model one's life on any one of these men and their ideas is therefore a matter of human choice, unrelated to religion as I am defining it. It has, in any case, to be asked how far any person who models his life on another is simply building an idealised image on the basis of (often disputed) historical evidence; either that, or he has simply visualised in the other the ideal which he has himself come to accept. (The varied images and interpretations of Jesus or Buddha over the centuries indicate that both have been fertile inspirers of this kind of idealism.) It seems, in any case, preferable to follow the existentialist emphasis on personal autonomy, if authentic living is to be experienced.

One comment must be added here with special reference to Christianity. There is a world of difference, at least on the face of it, between declaring oneself to be an imitator of Jesus and saying (with St Paul) 'Christ lives in me'. No Buddhist (though Zen speaks of achieving 'Buddha nature') or Jew, Hindu or Muslim would make a similar claim apropos of their spiritual founders, which means that either Christianity is unique, and Jesus actually was the incarnation of God who came back to life again after being dead for nearly two days or that Paul, along with others who make similar affirmations, was simply putting a human face on the mystical experience. Since the first alternative represents a myth whose worth has long been rejected even by many Christians, who view the Resurrection narrative as symbolic of the ultimate triumph of good over evil (although see Chapter 10 for a discussion of that dichotomy), we may accept the second interpretation. Paul's remarkable mystical statement gives visual expression to what Buddhists term 'sunyata', the void, and Hindus 'moksha', enlightenment, or *samadhi*, the union of the self with the ground of being. 'Christ within me' stands alongside (for instance) the experience of Buddha-nature, the Hindu realisation 'tat tvam asi', and the Chinese sense of harmony with the Tao. It illustrates the fact that, as has been stressed throughout, there are many paths to the ultimate religious experience, none of them being uniquely 'the true path'. I shall discuss later how this applies to those who do not feel any need at all for a specific signpost on the journey.

Just as the process of following a great teacher's example is irrelevant to religion, so also is the *exaltation of certain texts to the status of absolute truth*. Again this needs to be affirmed more adamantly with regard to the theistic religions than to the non-theistic; the Old and New Testaments and the Qur'an contain guidelines on experiencing the numinous, but, by a process similar to that whereby the Godhead becomes identified with God, the medium – to quote McLuhan out of context – through which these guidelines are conveyed has in the minds of many become irrevocably confused with the message. As we have already seen, both the Bible and the Qur'an contain a large amount of material which reflects the primitive views and values of the writers many centuries ago. A large number of these views are manifestly quite irrelevant to the twenty-first century, and there seems no sane reason, except for historical interest, why anybody should be expected to read them today. As it is there is much in these books which is distasteful, even repellent, and the reader's task is to separate the wheat from the chaff. The trouble is that too many then make a meal of the chaff, as scriptural fundamentalists throughout the world exemplify. The 'Holy' Bible, from the Pentateuch to the Apocalypse, has more salivating accounts of the destruction of God's so-called enemies than it has teaching of how to achieve a mystical experience; more ancient history than guidance on how to develop the spiritual consciousness; more parochialism than universality. There is real religion expressed among its pages, but one must be a biblical student to find it. Many of its stories have, for better or worse, become part of our Western culture, but that doesn't make the West any more religious. The *Tao Te Ching* is a book which expresses genuine religion more comprehensively than any of the scriptures produced by the Semites, but Taoists do not treat the book as though it were a religious icon. (One reason why I should like to be a guest on 'Desert Island Discs' is to be able to tell the interviewer, when she asks which book I should like to take, 'alongside the Bible and Shakespeare, which are already there', to start by removing the Bible and replacing it with this Chinese classic. If children in schools were encouraged to read and reflect on one of its pages every day, I believe that many more of them would come to understand the naturalness of the religious experience than will ever find it through bible study.)

Another piece of lumber to be cast overboard is *the association of religion with morals*. I discussed this matter in some detail in Chapter 10, so I will add just one further consideration. Christianity as a religion is defended and advocated, more, I suspect, than on any other grounds, on the basis of the morality which it allegedly inspires. 'Christian Ethics' is a choice in A-level Religious Education; courses are taught under this title at universities and colleges; books are written about it. The concept is, however, vacuous and, as reflected in much so-called Christian behaviour over the centuries, an oxymoron: *there is no such entity as Christian ethics*. The implication, often asserted by those who defend it, is that morality based on the teaching of Christ is somehow superior to that which springs from any other source. This is, of course, arrant and, as sometimes expressed, arrogant nonsense. It implies that Christians are more likely to live 'the good life' (whatever content be given to that question-begging phrase) than people of other religions or with no formal religious affiliation at all; and this is insulting to anyone, whether Buddhist, Taoist, humanist or atheist, who takes their values seriously and attempts to practise them widely.

The main problem with the assertion arises, however, when the attempt is made to establish the content of 'Christian ethics'. In a recent (2000) radio discussion, two intelligent people, one a regular BBC interviewer, the other a famous novelist who had just published a commentary on *Paul's Letter to the Romans*, both agreed that Paul was the inventor, or, as they expressed it, the discoverer of the Golden Rule: 'Love thy neighbour as thyself.' It is rare to meet a Christian who thinks otherwise; yet that verse is written, word for word, in Leviticus 18: 9, centuries before Paul arrived on the scene. The same sentiments are found in the writings of all the world's spiritual leaders, some from an atheistic viewpoint. Confucius expressed the Golden Rule in its (more universally applicable) negative form: 'Do not do to others what you would not wish them to do to you.' His successor, Mencius, said (VII.B.16):

> 'Benevolence' means 'man'. When these two are conjoined, the result is 'the Way'.

The Taoist, Chuang Tzu said (23):

> He who can find no room for others lacks fellow feeling, and to him who lacks fellow feeling, all men are strangers.

The Hindu Basavanna (*Vacana*, 247) wrote:

> What sort of religion can it be without compassion?
> You need to show compassion to all living beings.
> Compassion is the root of all religious faiths.

Christians are inclined to defend their uniqueness in this area with the affirmation that their faith alone teaches its adherents to love their *enemies*. They should turn to the *Tao Te Ching* (p. 63) and read:

> Do good to him who has done you an injury.

or to the Jewish Tosefta (*Baba Metzia*, 2.26):

> Aid an enemy before you aid a friend, to subdue hatred;

or to the Buddhist Dhammapada (223):

> Conquer anger by love. Conquer evil by good. Conquer the stingy by giving. Conquer the liar by truth;

or to the Hindu epic, *Ramayana* (Yuddha Kanda, 115):

> A superior being does not render evil for evil . . .
> One should never harm the wicked or the good or even criminals meriting death. A noble soul will ever exercise compassion even toward those who enjoy injuring others – for who is without fault?

(A cautionary note here was uttered by the typically laconic Confucius: 'If you love your enemy as much as your friend, what advantage is there in being a friend?)

Love, compassion, goodwill, empathy, however the impulse be termed, is, in fact, a thoroughly human feeling, and the behaviour associated with it is equally human. The same goes for any moral guidelines which emerge from the New Testament. Their significance lies not in the fact that Jesus invented them, but that, from the plethora of moral counsel from a wide range of sources, these were his emphases. The Sermon on the Mount (Matthew 5: 7) is, in fact, a magnificent description of the way of Zen, and it would be no belittling of Jesus to describe him as eminent in the tradition of Zen masters.

Sadly, in practice, Christian ethics has come to mean a far less open lifestyle than is advocated in those chapters. Anyone who opens his remarks with the phrase 'speaking as a Christian' almost invariably proceeds to oppose and denounce, as throughout history Christians have always denounced, any new development in science which hinges on human behaviour, especially sexual behaviour. When *in vitro* fertilisation was introduced, it was denounced as 'playing God'; likewise the discovery of the human genome, with its consequence that foetuses could be genetically modified in order to ensure healthier babies; likewise same-sex marriages; likewise giving homosexuals the same rights as heterosexuals; likewise abortion and euthanasia; it is, in fact, only relatively recently that women have been allowed pain relief in giving birth on the grounds of the statement in Genesis 3: 16, 'In sorrow shalt thou bring forth children'. Ironically, many of these people who are barriers to progress are in responsible positions, with the power and authority to impose their views on the many who wish to enjoy the benefits which science brings.

This is, however, a diversion from the key consideration, which is that morality and religion belong to two totally discrete areas of human experience. Religion is ultimately independent of God, charismatic figures, sacred writings and moral behaviour. All these, together with holy objects and buildings, are examples of forms or structures which, so people associated with them persuade themselves, allow them to assume that they are religious. But this is a delusion because, being human structures, they express the phenomena rather than the noumena of religion: 'the words fly up, the thoughts remain below'. Religion at its most sublime is substance rather than form, and the implications of that assertion must now be examined.

By describing religion in that way, I am aware that care must be taken over the meaning of the words, since they both have a wide range of connotations. By substance I mean essential nature or essence of anything; by form, its outward appearance, its image or representation (as opposed to the Platonic view of forms which is the ideal of which the actuality is an – inevitably – imperfect representation). An example from Christian theology illustrates the distinction. In the Nicene Creed, Jesus, the Son of God, is described as 'being of one substance with the Father'. St Paul describes him as 'taking the form of a servant . . . being found in human form' (Phil 2: 7/8). Within the limits provided by those two quotations, the distinction is clear; but one of them is quoted from a passage which illustrates the error which I was describing earlier. Prior to the words quoted, Paul had written (v. 6) of Jesus as having been 'in the form of God'. Paul was, admittedly, a theologian rather than a philosopher, but his lack of clarity exemplifies the confusion perfectly. Jesus may have shared God's substance (or, to use the term reached in Chapter 5, the Godhead's substance), but he could not have shared his form, since the Godhead has no form. If it had, it would be identifiable by human senses, recognisable to all. It is precisely because people in their multitudes follow Paul in thinking of God as having form that the word should be abandoned. Only then will many who do not view themselves as religious recognise that their disenchantment has arisen from alienation from the traditional forms, while *all along they may well have been experiencing the substance through other forms*, as exemplified in Chapter 9.

Those for whom empirical evidence is alone acceptable on any matter will view this concept of substance as vague and unreal. They may well scorn (some more scathingly than others) anyone's professed belief in a religious experience on the grounds that it is unverifiable – which is, of course, the case. This view is presented less frequently and with less conviction than it was half a century or more ago, when logical positivism ruled the roost in philosophical seminars, and verifiability was the be-all and end-all of intelligent discussion. Today, with atheists and agnostics openly acknowledging experiences which I am calling religious (even if that is not their word) this viewpoint is more muted. The fact is that if the religious experience is unreal, it follows that billions of people, from widely differing levels of existence and in a variety of contexts, have been deluding themselves by imagining that the euphoria or sense of absorption that they feel on certain occasions were something more than brain cells stimulated by one catalyst or another. Some may reduce the experiences to no more than the effects of matter in motion, but this still leaves open the possibility that the effects have been caused by a force in the universe which is other than physical: in other words, that there is a spiritual dimension alongside the material (the *purusha* and *prakriti* – spirit and nature – of sankya-yoga): substance as well as form.

The fact that the experience cannot be described is unimportant. How does one describe pain, euphoria, an orgasm – experiences shared by most of the human race, and therefore unchallenged by monistic materialists? How much more difficult it is, then, to describe one shared by many but, apparently, not by all? Foreshadowing Husserl's phenomenology, William James wrote (op. cit.):

> No one can make clear to another who has never had a certain feeling, in what the quality or worth of it consists. One must have musical ears to know the value of a symphony; one must have been in love oneself to understand a lover's state of mind.

To state, then, that religious experiences cannot be real because they have no form is to turn one's eyes from a fair proportion of human affirmations over the millennia. The scepticism is not only blind, however, but also inconsistent. Presumably monists do not deny the existence of time because it has no form; or of consciousness, or gravity, which have no form. Even our common experience of breathing air and living with electricity means that we are accepting as real entities without form. The fact that all people experience these and not all experience religion is beside the point. Not all people have musical ears, or are numerate, but this fact in no way diminishes the reality and worth of music or numeracy among those who can appreciate them. It has been suggested that some people have a 'religious gene' which is denied to others. My view is that, as with innumeracy, illiteracy, or tone-deafness, where, with patient guidance at the right speed, observable progress can be made towards their opposites, so, similarly, many more people can be enabled to recognise religious experiences as they occur. Whether religion is for all, it is impossible to tell. Hindus believe that all will eventually gain enlightenment, but their religion assumes an indefinite number of individual reincarnations for this to happen: I am viewing the question from the perspective of only one cycle of experience (see below on 'eternity now').

The issue remains as to whether absorption should be viewed as Hindus (and some Buddhists) describe it: union between the self and the ground of being (samadhi in Hinduism, nirvana, or sunyata, the void, in Buddhism) which are viewed as indicative of an eternal state; or whether it should be viewed as a bonus to be enjoyed temporarily, as oases in the desert. Bede Griffiths, in *Return to the Centre*, opted for the first condition:

> There is an experience of being in pure consciousness which gives lasting peace to the soul. It is an experience of the Ground or Depth of being in

the Centre of the soul, an awareness of the mystery of being beyond sense
or thought, which gives a sense of fulfilment, of finality, of absolute truth.

One can empathise with this description, but the question remains: is this an
account of a union between the individual self and the ground of being, or
is it the discovery of a higher self, latent in everybody, but overshadowed
(and perhaps extinguished?) in many by routine commitments and over-
concern for the yang aspect of life, as stars are made invisible by the artificial
lights of a city?

Perhaps in the end it does not matter because the descriptions are of the
same experience, viewed from different perspectives, like descriptions of a
mountain by, on the one hand, a poet and, on the other, a geologist. Here, for
example, are two descriptions of the religious experience, the first unambiguously interpreting it as a union of the self with the whole, the second as
a discovery of a higher self. The first is by Denys, Pseudo-Dionysius, writing
in *Mystical Theology*:

> It breaks forth, even from that which is seen and which sees, and plunges
> the mystic into the Darkness of Unknowing, whence all perfection of
> understanding is excluded, and he is enwrapped in that which is alto-
> gether intangible and noumenal, being wholly absorbed in Him who is
> beyond all.

The second is from Tennyson, and is a personal account of a religious experience (quoted in James, op. cit., p. 170). He describes how, since a child, he
had been able to enter into a 'trance' simply by silently repeating his own
name; then:

> all at once, as it were out of the intensity of consciousness of individu-
> ality, individuality itself seemed to dissolve and fade away into boundless
> being, and this not a confused state but the clearest, the surest of the
> surest, utterly beyond words – where death was an almost laughable
> impossibility – the loss of personality (if so it were) seeming no extinc-
> tion, but the only true life. I am ashamed of my feeble description. Have
> I not said the state is utterly beyond words?

Perhaps the twin states, of absorption in the ground of being, and of disso-
lution in boundless being are not dissimilar after all, so that Denys would
have welcomed Tennyson as a fellow sharer in enlightenment.

Eternity now

In what has gone before I have been deliberately non-committal on the issue
which, as evinced by every poll taken on the subject, most draws people to

religion and to the acknowledgement of belief in God: the unwillingness of humans to face up to the fact of extinction: of that which has being to come to terms with non-being, as Heidegger expressed that state of foreboding. He argued that it was this apprehensiveness which alone lent significance to human activity; that if we knew that we should live forever, nothing of any worth would ever be undertaken. 'Without anxiety,' he said, 'there can be no creativity.'

Manifestly, however, we shall not live forever: not on this earth anyway. The one certainty in life is that we shall die, along with every other living species that ever has lived or ever will. And even if we view death as the nat-ural finale to the inevitable diminution of our faculties, its starkness remains awesome. Apart from those who are dying of a painful disease who in the end long for release, most people, even in extreme old age, would still grab an extra twelve months if it were on offer.

It is by this fear that belief in an eternal God has been fostered more than by any other factor. The message which the theistic religions have pro-claimed over the centuries has therefore been that those who believe in him 'shall never die, but have everlasting life', as Jesus promised his followers. From this has followed the sense of need to be a true believer, an obedient servant, a loyal follower. God is in his heaven and, if we live as he requires of us, there we shall be with him, and with all the vast throng who have kept the faith, among whom, it is hoped, may be our own deceased loved ones.

This scenario is the theistic alternative to the doctrine of reincarnation taught in Hinduism. Since, however, people have no memory of previous existences, it seems wise not to bank any hope on re-entering the cycle (and in any case Hinduism teaches that the aim, through enlightenment (moksha) is to get off the cycle and enter samadhi). The theory of reincarnation has a pragmatic use, in that it removes the need for anyone to gain enlightenment during the present cycle of experience: other than that, it may serve as a com-fort for those who cannot face the thought that 'death closes all'.

The question to face is not so much whether belief in eternal existence is a sound belief (that is, one that can be justified from human experience, which it cannot – 'dead men come back never'), but whether there is any *point* in it. The average life-span on earth is a long time, but eternity puts it in the shade. What are we expected to do throughout eternity? Do we have spiritual bodies, and if so, will they change as our earthly bodies changed? And if they don't change, will they be identifiable with our earthly bodies? If so, at which period of our earthly bodies will they be fixed? These and many related questions indicate that most people who look forward to spending eternity in heaven simply have not thought through the conse-quences of that aspiration if it were fulfilled. (It is astonishing that some people look forward to it who do not know what to do with themselves on a wet Sunday afternoon.)

The answer from some quarters is that we enter into a different dimension from that which we presently experience. In this new dimension we are spirits rather than bodies, and time and location no longer exist: we are in a new state where there is no longer changefulness as in our present condition. Again this raises questions. The assumption, even behind this theory, is that in some way we retain self-consciousness: whatever it is that we are experiencing, we *are* experiencing. Yet, if we are no longer physical but spiritual, we will have lost all the organs and faculties which, in this life at any rate, are the requirement for those experiences. And if we have entered a state of absorption (in the ground of being, the void, the Tao, the Godhead) as I have suggested can occur in this present life, how can we know this when we do not, as in this present life, return afterwards to the normal waking state? Again the belief is riddled with difficulties.

It seems preferable by far to view the whole problem existentially, and recognise that the eternity we seek is being experienced now. I quoted on p. 33 the affirmation by the god Krishna to Arjuna in the *Bhagavad-gita*: 'There never was a time when I was not, and there never will be a time when I will not be.' It is important to keep our eyes on the 'I' in that sentence: the self-aware being of whom I am therefore conscious. Speaking personally (as is essential for this argument), there never was a time, as a simple matter of fact, when I was not conscious of being. I know *that* the universe has been in existence for about six billion years before my arrival on the scene, but *I* have not experienced these years. So far as *I* am concerned, they never happened: the universe began at my birth (or a little time after – whenever I became conscious of myself as a person); and the only universe there *is* is whatever presents itself as the object of my consciousness, whatever ideas, experiences, facts, relationships, values, beliefs, knowledge I have accumulated over my lifetime: that is the universe, and there never was a time when *I* was not aware of it. So while I know *that* there were aeons before I came into being, *I* have never not been. History began with my arrival – or just after.

The same perspective governs my view of the other end of the cycle. Just as there never was a time when I was not, so there never will be a time when *I* will not be. All that I shall know in this life is being; when I cease to be I shall not know it. So while I know *that* I shall die, *I shall never know death*. It is, in fact, a contradiction in terms. After my death, others will have to manage without me; but I shall not know that this is the case. With my death the universe will end, though I shall not know this. All I shall know, forever as far as my consciousness is concerned, is eternity: eternity now. *And I shall never know otherwise*. Others will know that I am dead; I shall never know it. Once I sink into the final coma before the end I shall by definition be unaware that this state has come upon me. Others may mourn my death, as I have mourned over others; but I shall never have to mourn for myself, since I shall always (that is, forever) be aware of that self through my consciousness.

To fear death and look for some kind of new life in some unimaginable world in a different dimension seems therefore to me pointless, even infantile. Of course there is sorrow, and a sense of loss, whenever death occurs. But the sorrows of death are the sorrows of the living, not of the dead. I weep over some people's deaths – especially those who die prematurely. I think of all that life might have offered them, which they will never experience. But it is I who weep, not they: they are in peace, the peace of what Buddha described as the 'blissful void'. Once this perspective has been gained (and it is through the writings of Martin Heidegger that I gained the tranquillity which this perspective brings), then death becomes no more than an experience which happens to others along the way, affecting me much or little, but just one of the many varieties of experience which anyone accummulates during his or her life. The losing of faculties as age advances is of course a matter for regret: but however feeble the body or mind, the fact of being remains, and with it the continuing experience of eternity. My death has no role in my life except as a goad to creative thinking and activity.

The whole concept is admirably expressed in a poem by Arthur Symons entitled 'Indian Meditation':

> Where shall this self at last find happiness?
> O Soul, only in nothingness.
> Does not the Earth suffice to its own needs?
> And what am I but one of the Earth's weeds?
> All things have been and all things shall go on
> Before me and when I am gone;
> This self that cries out for eternity
> Is what shall pass in me:
> The tree remains, the leaf falls from the tree.
>
> I would be as the leaf, I would be lost
> In the identity and death of frost,
> Rather than draw the sap of the tree's strength
> And for the tree's sake be cast off at length.
> To be is homage unto being; cease
> To be, and be at peace,
> If it be peace for self to have forgot
> Even that it is not.

The perspective which I have presented has two consequences in particular. The first is the total removal of any fear of death. The second is an absolute realisation of the superfluity of a God to guarantee another life after this one. So any attempt to link religion with the life beyond is doomed, with this perspective, to lose its *raison d'être*. The religion which I have been describing is for the eternity which is integral to the condition of being. Religion is for here and now; whether we shall find it a reality after our deaths may be an interesting subject of speculation, but is essentially irrelevant to the main issue.

The religious person in a post-modern age

God is dead: therefore theism is dead: therefore God-talk must cease. His image may continue to affect many lives for years to come, but those with ears to hear have heard, and moved on.

To what? The glib answer verbalised by critics of my thesis is that love for one's neighbour will disintegrate, since that love springs essentially from love of God. Loving God, they aver, means seeing him in one's neighbour, and therefore feeling at one with him: without the divine dimension the essential *worth* of the neighbour will be lost sight of. Belief in the brotherhood of man depends on belief in the fatherhood of God. As Hegel expressed it, the final stage of human relationships (what he termed the State but might better, according to Rowan Williams, be termed a Commonwealth) is one in which I recognise myself in others, because all of us are united in God.

That, at any rate, is the argument of those who maintain that theism is a valid interpretation of experience. It has two basic flaws. The first is the assumption that whenever this perspective has been dominant in society, good neighbourliness has followed. This assumption is historically groundless. To be sure, there never was a time when some theists did not aim to put this ideal into practice; but their numbers were always low in comparison with those whose lives were spent feathering their own nests, whether in this world or – so they hoped – in the next. The Middle Ages are known as the 'Age of Faith', but they were centuries in which every vice known to man was freely committed, often in the name of the Church, sometimes by its highest authorities.

The second fallacy in the theistic apologia is the assumption that those who have been godless have been unconcerned about their neighbours. Humanists over the centuries will justifiably decry this assumption. (The number of centuries under discussion is, of course, limited because it has been only in relatively recent times that a person has been free to declare himself an atheist or humanist and not suffer the wrath of the Church in consequence.) Of course, there have been self-seeking atheists, but the question that matters is whether their numbers, percentage-wise, have been higher than those of theists. Comparisons here are impossible, but present experience suggests that whether a person lives a 'good' life or not bears little or no relation to his or her theistic beliefs or lack of them.

The burden of this book, however, has not been about moral standards but religious experience. My concern is that we should extricate religion from the quagmire in which it has been interblended with theism. Some may say that this is a forlorn hope, since the two have become an alloy from which no single element can be extracted. I hope that enough evidence has been presented in the foregoing pages to suggest otherwise: godless religion has always been experienced among human beings, albeit often unwittingly, and I wish finally to give a pen-portrait of a religious person in a post-modern, post-god age, using, for convenience, the male pronoun.

The basic fact about him is that he is sympathetic to the view that there is a dimension in the universe which cannot be contained solely in its physical description. He may not necessarily call this a spiritual dimension (and he is certainly unlikely to use the term 'numinous'): but he will aver from his own experience that there are times when and places where he has, in a way that he finds difficult to describe, entered a state in which he has lost the sense of individuality and become absorbed in some other element. He has found that these experiences are rewarding and reinvigorating. They sometimes spark off a creative urge, sometimes inspire him to greater understanding of other people's values and interests, always leave him with a sense of wonder and a fuller appreciation of the riches of being alive. These experiences are probably the most important that he has, and he seeks out the contexts in which they occur as often as he can (which may be more, or less, often than others who encounter them).

The contexts of the experiences may vary from time to time, but some he is likely to find more rewarding than others. It may be through music, painting, literature or drama, any of which he will view not just (if at all) as a critic but as one who wishes to be absorbed in the particular expression of creativity. The occasions he will remember with most satisfaction will be those which provided him with moments when time and place cease to exist.

He will probably be a lover of nature, and will seek out particular places whenever he can: probably, as an urban dweller, finding these occasions too infrequent. He will view nature not just as something to be enjoyed as a thing of beauty, but, somehow, as a spirit with which to be engaged. He may prefer a forest at twilight, a glen at midday, a field or stretch of seascape in the early morning, a mountain peak, or the bend of a river. The time of the year will be unimportant: the land's frozen surface in the winter will speak to him as much as a field of wild flowers on a summer's day. Some places and times may become special, and he may go out of his way to be there on these occasions. To be alone is not essential, but some experiences, though he will try to describe them to others, will create a private resource, which will play an important part in his life's equilibrium.

His life will, as far as possible, be a balance between work and leisure: between commitments when his time is mortgaged and his particular skills are required, and involvements into which he chooses to enter when there are no external demands on him. These will include periods of quiet reflection, and he may pursue, on a regular basis, a particular method of meditation. Over time, he may find these periods increasingly absorbing, and that they play a major part in giving symmetry to his life. He will encourage his children to practise some form of yoga, and may advocate that it be introduced into their school curriculum. Without perhaps using the words, he will seek to pattern his life on the harmony and balance of the yin and yang.

He will not live his life in the expectation of a future life, but will view the world which he encounters as the arena of all that matters to give the present life meaning and purpose. For the rest he is prepared to wait and see – or not, as the case may be.

He will have built up habits of behaviour which he hopes are not too aggravating to others. Where necessary he will criticise certain behavioural patterns in others, but, on the whole, he appreciates the possibility that his values may not necessarily be theirs. Though he will be ready to express these values, he will not wish to force them on others. Regretfully, he will conclude that some forms of behaviour should not be countenanced in the community, and that the perpetrators must therefore be removed. But he will have no concept of a transformation of the world as it is to some kind of permanent utopian state; he will rather accept that, with all the natural tendencies to aggressive self-assertiveness which he encounters, the miracle is that the human race has still managed to survive. He will take action when the occasion compels it, but generally will let things take their natural course.

He will attend no place of worship, though he will not belittle those who do (though his attitude toward them may be like that which he would have to a man who boasts that his wife is beautiful and his children bright). He accepts that everybody lives by one myth or another, but thinks that the myth which underlies the beliefs and practices of these people is one that has served its time.

He hesitates to call himself a religious man because he is disenchanted, if not appalled, by the activities and ideas which he reads about as proceeding and being offered in the name of religion. He finds papal denunciations of various common expressions of sexuality as 'intrinsically evil' to be abhorrent, and the popular indulgence in fake frenzy in the more evangelical churches to be nauseating – a kind of religious masturbation. But he would agree that if to be religious is to be able to empathise with Browning when he wrote in 'Bishop Blougram's Apology':

> Just when we are safest, there's a sunset-touch
> A fancy from a flower-bell, someone's death,
> A chorus-ending from Euripides –
> And that's enough for fifty hopes and fears
> As old and new at once as Nature's self,
> To rap and knock and enter in our soul . . .

then he will accept the label in the hope that it will become more popularly used to describe the likes of himself than it has hitherto.

If this portrayal of the religious person of the post-modern age has any basis in reality, it raises enormous questions about the future of the theistic religions. It is impossible to generalise about this. In their fundamentalist expressions – whether catholic or biblical – they will continue indefinitely, I suppose, catering for those who seek an anchor in life, even one that requires them to throw their rational faculties overboard. The myths which underlie both of these forms of religion, like the myths of racial superiority or the objectivity of moral values, will continue to appeal until people more universally come of age. I hope that A. N. Wilson is wrong in his belief, expressed in an *Evening Standard* article, that the future lies not with Christianity, but with Islam, with the crescent rather than the cross. God is Allah, and God is dead.

Cupitt believes that the future of Christianity lies in its rejection of its myths, and the furtherance of its teaching as contained in the Sermon on the Mount and other passages in Mark's Gospel and the lost document on Jesus's teaching known as Q (from the German *Quelle*, meaning source). He suggests that these were the originals, and that all that is contained in John's Gospel, together with much of Matthew and Luke, are glosses added considerably later. In particular, this means rejecting the Birth and Resurrection narratives.

If Cupitt is right (and many agree he is), it implies that Christianity must drop its claim to be the 'true' religion of the world, but take its place alongside other religions in offering guidance on how to cope with life and live harmoniously alongside others. The problem here, as I illustrated on p. 128, is that on these issues Christianity has nothing to add to what others have stated. That being the case, its main role may well be as a catalyst in the discovery of a world ethic, in the foundation of which the theologian Hans Kung is the guiding light. Even with that concession, however, one is bound to ask what the point is of trying to discover a 'world ethic'. As I suggested in Chapter 10, the way to live alongside others is more likely to be the natural way of Tao than any new form of the Ten Commandments.

So what remains? I have tried to indicate that religion remains if it is understood as the experience, via one route or another, of the numinous: the mystical experience. One could describe it as oneness with, or absorption in, the infinite. However one describes it, it is real, and a force for enrichment in, potentially, everybody's life. As Gandhi said, religion is to be found in everybody, though many are unconscious of it. Dietrich Bonhoeffer argued from prison that people cannot afford to be religious any more. He was reacting *in extremis* to the old view of religion. Perhaps the understanding of it which I have described will encourage the view that religion is in fact an innate, exhilarating faculty in human beings, with the capacity always to elevate, sometimes to inspire.

Select bibliography

The place of publication in all cases is London unless otherwise stated.

Abe, M., *Zen and Western Thought* – Macmillan 1985.
Addiss, T. S. and Lombard, S., *Tao Te Ching – Lao Tzu* – Hacket 1993.
Alston, W. P., *Philosophy of Language* – Prentice-Hall, New Jersey 1964.
Altizer, T., *The Gospel of Christian Atheism* – Collins 1967.
Ancelet-Hustache, J., *Master Eckhart* – Longman, Harlow 1957.
Armstrong, K., *The English Mystics* – Kyle Cathie 1991.
——, *A History of God* – Heinemann 1993.
——, *The Battle for God*: *Fundamentalism in Judaism, Christianity and Islam* – HarperCollins 2000.
Barrett, W., *Irrational Man* – Heinemann 1961.
Bierce, A., *The Devil's Dictionary* – Wordsworth 1996.
Billington, R. J., *Living Philosophy* – Routledge 2nd edn 1994.
——, *East of Existentialism* – Routledge 1990.
——, *Understanding Eastern Philosophy* – Routledge 1997.
Blofeld, J., *Beyond the Gods: Taoist and Buddhist Mysticism* – London 1974.
Boyer, P., *Religion Explained* – Heinemann 2000.
Buber, M., *I and Thou* – T. & T. Clark 1958.
Capra, Fritjof, *The Tao of Physics* (various editions).
Carr, B. and Mahalingam, I. (eds), *Companion Encyclopedia of Asian Philosophy* – Routledge 1997.
Carter, J. R. and Palihawadana, M. (trans), *The Dhammapada* – Oxford University Press, Oxford 1987.
Chan, W-T., *A Source Book in Chinese Philosophy* – Princeton University Press, New Jersey 1963.
Chang, J., *The Tao of Love and Sex* – Wildwood House 1977.
Chatterjee, M., *Gandhi's Religious Thought* – Notre Dame de Paris, Paris 1983.
Clark, J. M. and Skinner, J. (trans.) *Meister Eckhart* – HarperCollins 1958.
Clarke, J. J. (ed.), *Nature in Question: An Anthology of Ideas and Arguments* – Earthscan Publications 1993.
——, *Jung and Eastern Thought* – Routledge 1994.
——, *Oriental Enlightenment* – Routledge 1997.
——, *The Tao of the West* – Routledge 2000.

Cleary, T., *The Essential Tao* – Harper, San Francisco 1991.

Colegrave, S., *Yin und Yang* [German trans of *The Spirit of the Valley*] – Bern 1980.

Collins, S., *Selfless Persons* – Cambridge University Press, Cambridge 1982.

Copleston, F., *A History of Philosophy* – Doubleday, New York, 1985.

Cox, H., *The Secular City* – Doubleday, New York 1965.

Craig, W. (ed.), *Encyclopedia of Philosophy* – Routledge 1998.

Cupitt, D., *The Sea of Faith* – BBC 1984.

——, *Taking Leave of God* – SCM 1985.

——, *After God* – Weidenfeld & Nicolson 1997.

Desmond, A. and Moore, J., *Darwin* – Michael Joseph 1991.

Dissanayake, E., *Homo Aestheticus: Where Art Comes from and Why* – Free Press, New York 1992.

Dundas, P., *The Jains* – Routledge 1992.

Egner, R. E. and Denonn, L. E. (eds), *The Basic Writings of Bertrand Russell* – Routledge 1992.

Eliade, M., *The Sacred and the Profane: The Nature of Religion* – Harcourt Brace, New York 1959.

Feng, J. and English, G-F., *Tao Te Ching* – Wildwood House 1973.

Feuerbach, L., *The Essence of Christianity* – Harper Bros, New York 1957.

Fingarette, H., *Confucius: The Secular as Sacred* – Harper & Row 1972.

Foy, W. (ed.) *The Religious Quest* – Routledge 1988.

Frazer, J. G., *The Golden Bough: A Study of Magic and Religion* – Macmillan 3rd edn 1911.

Fromm, E., *Man for Himself* – Routledge 1990.

Gandhi, M., *My Religion* – Bombay 1955.

Gellner, E., *Postmodernism, Reason and Religion* – Routledge 1992.

Gombrich, R., *Theravada Buddhism* – Routledge 1988.

Graham, A. C., *ChuanQ-Tzu, the Inner Chapters* – Unwin 1981.

Griffiths, Bede, *Return to the Centre* – Collins 1976.

Harvey, P., *Introduction to Buddhism* – Cambridge University Press, Cambridge 1990.

Heidegger, M., *Poetry, Language, Thought* (trans A. Hofstadter) – Harper & Row 1971.

Hick, J., *God has Many Names* – Westminster 1982.

——, *The Fifth Dimension* – Oneworld, Oxford 1999.

Hiriyanna, M., *Essentials of Indian Philosophy* – HarperCollins 1985.

Hollingdale, R. J. (ed.), *A Nietzsche Reader* – Penguin 1977.

Hospers, J., *Introduction to Philosophical Analysis* – Routledge & Kegan Paul 1956.

Hume, D., *Dialogues Concerning Natural Religion* (1779) – many modern editions.

Humphrey, N., *Leaps of Faith: Science, Miracles, and the Search for Supernatural Considerations* – Basic Books, New York 1992.

Husserl, E., *The Crisis of European Science and Transcendental Phenomenology* – Evanston, Illinois 1970.

Huxley, A., *The Perennial Philosophy* – Chatto & Windus 1946.

Huxley, T. H., 'Nature: Aphorisms by Goethe', in *Nature* – 1869.

Isherwood, C. (ed.), *Vedanta for the Western World* – Allen & Unwin 1948.

Jacobs, L. (ed.), *The Jewish Mystics* – Jerusalem 1976.

James, W., *The Varieties of Religious Experience* – Fontana 1960.

Johnson, W. (trans), *Bhagavad Gita* – Oxford University Press, Oxford 1994.

Johnston, W., *The Inner Eye of Love* – Harper & Row 1978.

Jung, C. G., *Modern Man in Search of a Soul* – Routledge & Kegan Paul 1959.

Katz, S. T. (ed.), *Mysticism and Philosophical Analysis* – Oxford University Press, Oxford 1978.

Kaufmann, W., *The Gay Science* – New York 1974.

Kee, A., *The Way of Transcendance* – Penguin 1971.

Keightley, A., *Into Every Life a Little Zen Must Fall* – Wisdom 1986.

Kenny, A., *Aquinas* – Oxford University Press, Oxford 1980.

King, Ursula, *Towards a New Mysticism* – Collins 1980.

——, *The Spirit of One Earth* – Paragon House, New York 1989.

Kovacs, G., *The Question of God in Heidegger's Phenomenology* – North Western University Press, Evanston, Illinois 1990.

Krell, D. F. (ed.), *Martin Heidegger: Basic Writings* – Harper & Row 1977.

Kwok, M-H., Palmer, M. and Ramsay, J., *Tao Te Ching* – Element 1993.

Lau, D. C., *Lao-Tzu: Tao Te Ching* – Penguin 1963.

——, *Mencius* – Penguin 1970.

Levine, M. P., *Pantheism: A Nonotheistic Concept of Deity* – Routledge 1992.

Lyon, D., *Postmodernity* – Open University Press, Milton Keynes 1994.

Malcolm, N., *Wittgenstein: A Religious Point of View* – Routledge 1993.

Matthiessen, P., *The Snow Leopard* – Picador 1979.

Mitchell, S., *Tao Te Ching* – Frances Lincoln 1999.

Needham, J., *Science and Civilisation in China* (5 vols) – Cambridge University Press, Cambridge 1965.

Nietzsche, F., *Thus Spake Zarathustra* – Worsdworth 1997.

Olivelle, P. (trans), *Upanishads* – Oxford University Press, Oxford 1996.

Otto, R., *Mysticism East and West* – Meridian, New York 1957.

——, *The Idea of the Holy* – Oxford University Press, Oxford 1958.

Palmer, M., *The Elements of Taoism* – Element 1991.

Pirsig, R., *Zen and the Art of Motorcycle Maintenance* – 1974.

Radhakrishnan, S., and Moore, *A Source Book in Indian Philosophy* – Princeton University Press, New Jersey 1957.

——, *Indian Philosophy* (2 vols) – Allen & Unwin 1977.

Rawson, P. and Legeza, L., *Tao: The Eastern Philosophy of Time and Change* – Thames & Hudson 1973.

Reed, D., *The Tao of Health, Sex and Longevity* – Simon & Schuster, New York 1989.

Richards, G. (ed.), *A Source Book of Modern Hinduism* – Curzon 1985.

Rider Encyclopedia of Eastern Philosophy and Religion – Random House 1989.

Roberts, D. E., *Existentialism and Religious Belief* – Oxford University Press, Oxford 1957.

Robinson, J., *Honest to God* – SCM 1963.

——, *Explorations into God* – SCM 1967.

Santoni, R. E. (ed.), *Religious Language and the Problem of Religious Knowledge* – Indiana University Press, Bloomington 1968.

Schumacher, E. F., *Small is Beautiful* – Abacus 1974.

Scruton, R., *A Short History of Modern Philosophy: From Descartes to Wittgenstein* – Routledge 1995.

Shearer, A., *Effortless Being: The Yoga Sutras of Patanjali* – Wildwood House 1982.

Sinha, I., *Tantra: the Cult of Ecstasy* – Hamlyn 1993.

Smart, N., *The Religious Experience of Mankind* – Scribners, New York 1983.

——, *Religion and the Western Mind* – State University of New York Press, New York 1987.

——, *World Religions* – Routledge 1999.

Solomon, M., *Beethoven* – Schirmer Books, New York 1977.

Spinoza, B. de, *Ethics* (trans S. Shirley, ed. S. Feldman) – Hackett Publishing Co., Indianapolis 1992.

Streng, F., *Emptiness: A Study in Religious Meaning* – Abingdon, New York 1967.

Suzuki, D. T., *Introduction to Zen Buddhism* – Rider 1949.

——, *Living by Zen* – Rider 1951.

——, *Zen and Japanese Buddhism* – Chas E. Tuttle Co. 1958.

——, *The Essentials of Zen Buddhism* – New York 1962.

——, Fromm, E. and De Martino, R., *Zen Buddhism and Psychoanalysis* – New York 1960.

Sze, M., *The Tao of Painting* – Princeton University Press, New Jersey 1963.

Tagore, R., *The Religion of Man* – Unwin 1970.

Teilhard de Chardin, P., *The Phenomenon of Man* – Collins 1959.

Tessier, L. J. (ed.), *Concepts of the Ultimate* – Macmillan 1989.

Underhill, E., *Mysticism* – Oneworld, Oxford, 1993.

Vivekananda, S., *Jnana Yoga* – Advaia Asram, Calcutta 1955.

——, *What Religion Is* – Advaia Asram, Calcutta 1977.

Waley, A., *The Way and its Power* – Allen & Unwin 1934.

——, The Analects of Confucius – Union 1988.

Watts, A., *The Way of Zen* – Penguin 1962.

——, *Tao: The Watercourse Way* – Arkana 1975.

Weil, Simone, *The Need for Roots* – Routledge & Kegan Paul 1957.

Whitehead, A. N., *Process and Reality* – Cambridge University Press, Cambridge 1929.

Wilson, A. N., *God's Funeral* – John Murray 1999.

Wilson, Williams, Sugarman, *Introduction to Moral Education* – Penguin 1967.

Wu, Laurence C., *Fundamentals of Chinese Philosophy* – University Press of America 1986.

Yu-Lan, Fung, *History of Chinese Philosophy* – Princeton University Press, New Jersey 1953.

Yutang, Lin, *The Importance of Living* – Heinemann 1938.

Zaehner, R. C., *Mysticism: Sacred and Profane* – London 1957.

Zimmer, H., *Philosophies of India* – Princeton University Press, New Jersey 1951.

Index

absolutism, moral 117
absorption, self into the divine, 60, 64–5, 122, 131–2, 139; *see also* samadhi
Advaita Vedanta 11–12, 16, 61–6, 72, 91, 108, 122
agnostics 130
ahimsa 87
Al-'Arabi 54
Allah 4, 139
Alston, W.P. 11 ff
Altizer, T. 2
Amiel 95
Analects of Confucius 14, 87
animism 20–2, 25
Anselm, St 33, 36–7, 65–6, 103–4
Aquinas 1, 33, 55
Aristotle 33, 55
Armstrong, K. 2, 27–8, 49
art: and beauty 93–4; as religion 94–7, 137
artist, as priest 93
atheism, atheists 128, 130, 136
Atman 11, 16, 63–5, 69, 81, 85
Augustine of Hippo 55, 123
Aurobindo, Ghose 100

Bacon, F. 43–4
Basavanna 128
Beethoven, L. 6, 94
Berkeley, G. 1
Bevan, A. 5
beyond good and evil 50, 57, 116–18, 121–3; *see also* good
beyond in the midst 6, 96, 106–7
Bhagavad-gita 24, 26, 33, 59, 60, 64, 73, 134

Bible: as God's word 13–14, 127; *pace* Denys 51; and Zen 74
Binyon, L. 96
Blake, Peter 93
Blake, William 93–4, 100, 111
Bodhidharma 72, 75, 79–80
Boethius 49
Bonhoeffer, D. 6, 96, 139
Booth, W. ix
Brahman 12, 16, 24, 26, 59–60, 62–5, 69–70, 72, 81, 85, 131
Browning, R. 138
Buber, M. 17, 40, 105–7
Buddha 67–8, 72, 126
Buddha-nature 126
Buddhism 5, 11, 13–16, ch 7 *passim*, 90, 121, 128
Bunuel, L. 1
Butler, S. 5

Camus, A. 31
Capra, F. 56
Carlyle, T. 9
Chardin, Teilhard de 29–30
charismaticism 7
Chesterton, G.K. 7, 53, 56–8
Ch'i 80–2, 87
Christian ethics *see* ethics
Christianity 11, 22, 47, 126–7
Chryssides, G. 81–2
Chuang-tzu 83–4, 89, 92, 118, 128
Coleridge, S.T. 104
Collins, S. 69
Confucianism *see* Confucius
Confucius 11, 13–14, 16, 87, 89–90, 92, 121, 128–9
conscience, as voice of God 3
Copernicus 3

Copleston, F.J. 37
cosmological argument 33–4
Cox, H. 105
cults 7
Cupitt, D. 2, 6, 92, 96, 111, 122–3,
    125, 139

Darwin, C. 3, 98–9, 126
De Nerval, G. 2
death of God 1–2, 105, 118, 125
deism 18–19
Denys 51–2, 55–6, 132; his
    classification of mystics 54–5
Descartes, R. 15, 36
Devil's Dictionary 36
dharma 13, 73
Dharmapadha 14, 68, 76, 129
Diener, M. 76–7
Dionysius, Pseudo- *see* Denys
ditheism *see* dualism
Donne, J. 48
dualism: 23–4; between God and man
    60; and death *see* eternity, individual

Eckhart, Meister 50, 52–3, 57, 59, 64,
    81, 87, 122
Einstein, A. 42
Ellis, Havelock 108
enlightenment *see* moksha
eternity, individual 4, 32–6, 65–6, 71,
    80
ethics: Christian 127–9; world 139
evil, intrinsic 138
evil, problem of 41
evolution 98–9
existentialism 50, 70, 76, 83–4

fetish 21
Feuerbach, L. 29
Fisher, H.A.L. 36
football, as a religion 12
form *see* substance
four states in Advaita Vedanta 61–3
fourth, the *see* turiya
Freud, S. 3, 6
Fromm, E. 1 06
fu 84
fundamentalism: biblical 4, 17, 126;
    ecclesiastical 139

gaia hypothesis 104
Galileo 3

Gandhi, M. 55, 122, 139
Gaunilo 37
genetics 3
God: imminent/transcendent 19, 22, 25;
    attributes of 26–30; 'proofs' 33–40;
    answer to human inadequacies 40–4;
    'levels' of belief in 47–50; as 'good'
    109–10; channels of his revelation
    114–15; as a human construct 125;
    superfluous 135
Godhead x, 52, 59, 64, 81, 91, 100,
    125, 127, 130, 134
Goethe 95, 99
golden rule 128–9
golden thread in history 35–6
good: its vagueness 109–10; and evil
    115–18
ground of being *see* Brahman
Griffith, B. 131–2

haiku 77–8, 85
Hegel, F. 36, 136
Heidegger, M. 2, 38, 64, 109, 125,
    135
Heine, H. 95
henotheism 22
Heraclitus 116
Hick, J. 51, 53–4, 59
Hinayana *see* Theravada
Hinduism: 5, 13–14, 16, 26, 50, ch 6
    passim, 73, 76, 90, 116, 125–6, 131;
    many gods 24; systems 61; beyond
    good and evil 121
Hobbes, T. 1
Holloway, R. 8, 13, 112, 133
Holy Communion 13
Honest to God 2, 10, 40
Hood, T. 101
Hospers, J. 48–9, 93
hsien *see* immortals
Hui-neng 67, 73–4
humanism 128–9, 136
Hume, D. 23, 34, 45, 112
Husserl, G. 131
Huxley, A. 56
Huxley, J. 29

I and thou 17, 104–8
icons, religious 125–6
Idea of the Holy 21
Ignatius Loyola 55, 57
illusion *see* maya

'immortals' 79–80
intuition: in Zen 72–3, 75–6; in Taoism
    80, 82, 85
Islam 11, 22, 47, 139

Jainism 11, 15–16, 51, 70, 87
James, W. 24, 48, 50, 131–2
Jesus 126, 129–30, 133
jiva 16
John of the Cross 54
Judaism 11, 22, 47
Julian of Norwich 54
Jung, C.G. 9, 23, 122, 126

Cabbala 53–4
Kant, I.l, 34, 36–9, 111–12
Keats, J. 5, 94, 100
Key, A. 2
Kierkegaard, S. 2, 50, 57, 76
Knox, J. 113
koan 75, 85
Kohlberg, L. 53–4
Kung, H. 139

Lao-tzu 81
Lawrence, D.H. 107
Leibniz, G. 48, 98
Lewis, C.S. 110, 112
literature as religion 95–6, 137
logical positivism 130–1
logos 82
lumber see hindrances

McLuhan, M. 127
Mahabharata 24, 26, 59
Mahayana Buddhism 68, 76, 125
mana 21
Marcus Aurelius 15
marks of existence in Buddhism 68–9
Marx, K. 126
maya 5
meditation: 15, 137–8; Buddhist 70–1
Meher Baba 122
Mencius 128
Mencken, H.L. 125
metaphysics: reality of 17, 124; without
    theology 77
Michelangelo 94
Mill, J.S. 113
Milton, J. 120
miracles 44–5
moksha 12–13, 62, 86, 122, 126, 133

Molière 93
monolatry 22
monotheism 22, 25–7
Moore, H. 6
moral argument 38–40
moral education 120–1
moral maturity 115–18, 118–20
morality: God-given 13–14; non-
    absolute 121–2
Mortimer, J. 101
Moses 125
Mozart 95
Muhammed 125–6
Mumon Ekai 73–4
music as religion 6, 94–5, 137
Mussolini, B. 5
mysterium tremendum 21
mystery 11, 43, 45, 85, 87, 90, 95–6,
    103, 107, 139
mysticism: 8, 26, 81, 86, 90, 96;
    Christian 49–58; Judaic/Islamic 53;
    in nature 100, 102; in mathematics
    102–3; in science 103; hindrances to
    (Zen) 72–6
myth: of God 125, 138–9; of the Son of
    God 82

Nagarjuna 68
Nanak 122
naturalness in Taoism 81, 83, 87,
    89–90
nature: as religion 6, 86, 98–102, 137;
    as mystical 99–104
neoplatonism 51
New Age 7, 104
New Testament: Matthew 115, 129;
    Luke 48; John 65, 82; four Gospels
    139; Romans 128; I Corinthians 34,
    42; Philippians 130; I Timothy 57;
    Revelation 115
Newton, I. 99
Nicene Creed 130
Nietzsche, F. 1–2, 7–8, 23, 50, 74, 76,
    89, 116
nirvana 16, 69–70, 95, 100, 131
noble eightfold path 71–2
non-dualism see advaita vedanta
noosphere 29–30
noumena III, 130
numinous 21, 25–6, 97, 127, 137, 139

Ockham, William of 1

Odo of Cluny 104
Old Testament: Genesis 21, 27, 41, 82, 129; Exodus 22, 114; Leviticus 42, 57, 114–15, 128; Numbers 21; Joshua 44
OM 62, 64
ontological argument 36–8
ontology and the individual 43, 66
Origin of Species 3–4
Otto, R. 21, 25
Ovid 11

painting *see* art
Pali Canon *see* Dharmapada
panentheism 25
pantheism 19–20
Parrinder, G. 24
Patourel, John Le 21
Paul, St 27, 34, 57, 103, 113, 126, 128, 130
phenomena 34, 111–130
phenomenology 48, 116–18, 131
philosophical Taoism *see* tao chia
Pirsig, R. 103
Planck, M. 103
Plato: x, 96, 102–3; and forms 130
Plotinus 51
polytheism 24–5, 47
Pope, A. 104
post-modernism: 115–23; and the religious person 137–9
prayer 15
process theology 29–30
p'u 84–5
Pure Land Buddhism 68
purusha-prakriti 131
Pythagorus 102–3

Quakers 12–13
Qur'an 54, 57, 115, 127

Radhakrishnan, S. 61
Ramakrishna 122
Ramayana 26, 59, 129
Rawson, P. 80
reincarnation 11, 62, 133
relativism 117–18
religion: as natural 7; unconscious 9; definition 10; characteristics 10–17; 3 types of 25–6; in painting 87, 93–4, 96; in music 94–5; in literature 95; sacred/profane 91–3; centred on a

person, invalidity of 111, 125–6; and morality, the alleged link 112–15, 127; 'lumber' in 124–9; universality of 131
religious taoism *see* tao chiao
resurrection myth 139
Rinzai school 74–5
ritual, danger of 13, 73
Robinson, J. 2, 25, 40, 42, 45, 105, 108
Robinson, Ruth 106
Russell, B. 1, 32, 35, 40

Salvation Army *see* Booth, W.
samadhi 62, 94, 97, 99–100, 126, 131, 133
Sankya-yoga *see* purusha-prakriti
Santayana, G. 92, 94, 103
Sartre, J-P. 2, 70, 84, 118
sat-chit-ananda 63, 65, 122
satori 72–3, 75–8, 85–7, 94, 97, 100
Savonarola 102, 107
Schopenhauer, A. 34
Scotus, Duns 1
Sea of Faith 2, 6
Sermon on the Mount 129, 139
sex as religion 88
Shakespeare 101–2
Shankara, Adi 59, 61–5, 72, 97
Shelley, P.B. 20, 52, 92, 96
Shiva 59
Smart, Ninian 64, 77
Smith, W.C. 10
Soto school 75
Spinoza, B. 1, 19
Stevenson, R.L. 32
substance, not form 130–2
suchness *see* tzu-yan
sunyata *see* void
Symonds, A. 135

tabu 21
Tagore 122
Taize community 89
tantrism 80, 107
Tao Te Ching 14, 17, 49, 51, 58, 77, 79, 81–5, 88–90, 127–8
tao-chia 80–5, 90
tao-chiao 79–80, 89–90, 107–8
taoism: 5, 11, 13–15, 76–7, ch 8 *passim*, 91, 96, 100, 102, 116, 121, 126, 128, 132, 134, 139; and painting 86–7

tat tvam asi 16, 26, 60, 65, 99, 126
te 81–3, 96
teleological argument 34–6
Ten Commandments 139
Tennyson, A. 3, 35, 97, 99, 103
theism: 22, 47–9, 60, 90; and nature 98, 136
Theravada Buddhism 11, 68–72, 77, 91
Thomajan, P.J. 93
Tillich, P. 83
Tolstoy, L. 107
Tosefta 128–9
transcendental state 96–7
turiya 62–3, 97, 108
tzu-yan 85

Underhill, E. 53
Upanishads 26, 59, 63–5
Ussher, Archb. 34

vagueness 56–7, 70, 93, 109, 130
Vedas 14, 26, 59
verifiability 130
Victorian values 113–14
Vishnu 59
Vivekananda 108, 122

void, the 78, 91, 100, 122, 126, 131, 134–5
Voltaire 18, 42, 98

Watts, A. 90
Wesley, J. 67, 74
Whitehead, A.N. 29
Whitman, Walt 117
Wilde, Oscar 11
Williams, Rowan 136
Wilson, A.N. 2–3, 92, 139
Wilson, J. 119
Wittgenstein, L. 7, 58, 88
Wordsworth, W. 6, 87, 100–1
wu-wei 83–4, 118

yin–yang: 15, 24, 80, 82–3, 86–7, 116–18, 121, 132; and sex 87–8
yoga 14, 55, 59, 63, 80, 138
Yoga Sutras of Patanjali 59
Young, Baroness 120

zazen 72, 74, 77
zen 12–13, 68, 72–8, 85–6, 91, 94, 121, 126, 129
Zoroastrianism 23